The bastard

they pillage our homeland, fields,
gardens and all, and we write poems about
flowers and trees.

They pillage our buildings, and we write
poems about sidewalks.

They pillage our possessions and gold, and
we write poems about beggars.

They pillage our factories, and we write
poems about workers.

They pillage our reality, and we write
poems about imagination.

Abderrahim Elkhassar
Moroccan poet

The 2016 Saif Ghobash Banipal Prize for Arabic Literary Translation

There are 19 eligible entries for the 2016 prize: 17 fiction and 2 poetry.

The 18 translators are: Kareem James Abu-Zeid, Ruth Ahmedzai Kemp, Nesreen Akhtarkhavari and Anthony A Lee, Roger Allen, T M Aplin, Charis Bredin and Emily Danby, Nicole Fares, Russell Harris, Michelle Hartman, William M Hutchins (3), Abdulwahid Lu'lu'a, Melanie Magidow, Nancy Roberts, Jonathan Smolin, Karim Traboulsi, and Jonathan Wright (2).

Confessions by Rabee Jaber, translated by Kareem James Abu-Zeid (New Directions, USA)

The Bride of Amman by Fadi Zaghmout, translated by Ruth Ahmedzai Kemp (Signal 8 Press, Hong Kong)

Desert Sorrows by Tayseer al-Sboul, translated by Nesreen Akhtarkhavari and Anthony A Lee (Michigan State University Press, USA)

My Torturess by Bensalem Himmich, translated by Roger Allen (Syracuse University Press, USA)

Hurma by Ali al-Muqri, translated by T M Aplin (Darf Publishers, UK)

Ebola '76 by Amir Tag Elsir, translated by Charis Bredin and Emily Danby (Darf Publishers, UK)

32 by Sahar Mandour, translated by Nicole Fares (Syracuse University Press, USA)

The Automobile Club of Egypt by Alaa Al Aswany, translated by Russell Harris (Canongate, UK)

Ali and his Russian Mother by Alexandra Chreiteh, translated by Michelle Hartman (Interlink Publishing, USA)

Telepathy by Amir Tag Elsir, translated by William M Hutchins (Bloomsbury Qatar Foundation Publishing, Qatar)

The Scarecrow by Ibrahim al-Koni, translated by William M Hutchins (CMES, University of Texas at Austin, USA)

A Portal in Space by Mahmoud Saeed, translated by William M Hutchins (CMES, University of Texas at Austin, USA)

All Faces but Mine by Samih al-Qasim, translated by Abdulwahid Lu'lu'a (Syracuse University Press, USA)

Mortal Designs by Reem Bassiouney, translated by Melanie Magidow (AUC Press, Egypt/USA)

The Dust of Promises by Ahlem Mostaghanemi, translated by Nancy Roberts (Bloomsbury Publishing, UK)

Whitefly by Abdelilah Hamdouchi, translated by Jonathan Smolin (Hoopoe Fiction, Egypt/USA)

The Holy Sail by Abdulaziz al-Mahmoud, translated by Karim Traboulsi (Bloomsbury Qatar Foundation Publishing, Qatar)

The Bamboo Stalk by Saud Alsanousi, translated by Jonathan Wright (Bloomsbury Qatar Foundation Publishing, Qatar)

The Televangelist by Ibrahim Essa, translated by Jonathan Wright (Hoopoe Fiction, Egypt/USA)

THE JUDGES: Paul Starkey (Chair), Emeritus Professor & winner of the 2015 prize; **Lucy Popescu**, author and journalist; **Zahia Smail Salhi**, lecturer and translator; **Bill Swainson**, editor and literary consultant.

BANIPAL
Magazine of Modern Arab Literature

●● **BRITISH**
●● **COUNCIL**

The Banipal Visiting Writer Fellowship

St Aidan's College of the University of Durham and Banipal magazine of modern Arab literature, with the support of the British Council, are establishing an annual writing fellowship for a published author writing in Arabic, based each year at St Aidan's College. The Banipal Visiting Writer Fellowship will be a three-month residency.

The Fellowship is based on the three cornerstones that have formed the core of Banipal magazine: that Arab literature is an essential part of world culture and human civilisation; that dialogue between different cultures needs to be continually deepened; and that the joy and enlightenment to be gained from reading beautiful poetry and imaginative writing is an integral part of human existence.

The Fellowship will encourage dialogue with the Arab world through literature. The cultural exchange and dialogue that it will enable, and create, will open windows for non-Arab audiences in the UK onto the realities of Arab cultures in all their diversity and vibrancy, enabling fruitful discourse to develop. It is hoped that this will lead to further exchange, to mutual respect, to new writings, to deeper understanding, and to contributing to Arab literature taking its rightful place in the canon of world literature.

Each year the Fellowship will provide a unique space for a published author writing in Arabic to reflect and to write, and to also have the opportunity to share their work with British audiences.

The British Council welcomes the creation of this opportunity for a published writer in Arabic to spend a significant amount of time in the UK, form connections with the British writing, translation and publishing communities, and share their work with the British public. The Fellowship will raise the profile of Arabic writing in the UK in general and the Council looks forward to the establishment of long-lasting connections between writers in the UK and the Arabic-speaking world.

The Fellowship will provide return travel costs to St Aidan's College from the Fellow's home, full board and accommodation in the College for the duration of the residency, and an honorarium of £1500.

The first Fellowship will take place from 23 January 2017 to 21 April 2017.

Applicants for this first Fellowship should submit, to the Principal of St Aidan's College, a letter of application and curriculum vitae that includes details of their published works and works in progress. Applications can be made by email or by post. The deadline for receiving applications for the first year's Fellowship in 2017 is 5pm UK time, Wednesday 30 November 2016. The successful applicant for the first Fellowship will be notified by email on Monday 19 December.

The selection panel:
Susan F Frenk, Principal, St Aidan's College, University of Durham;
Fadia Faqir, Creative Writing Fellow, St Aidan's College;
Samuel Shimon, Editor-in-chief, Banipal magazine;
Margaret Obank, Publisher, Banipal magazine

Postal address:
The Principal, St Aidan's College, University of Durham,
Windmill Hill, Durham DH1 3LJ, UK

Email address: Banipalfellowship@gmail.com

BANIPAL

Magazine of Modern Arab Literature

Banipal, founded in 1998, takes its name from Ashurbanipal, last great king of Assyria and patron of the arts, whose outstanding achievement was to assemble in Nineveh, from all over his empire, the first systematically organised library in the ancient Middle East. The thousands of clay tablets of Sumerian, Babylonian and Assyrian writings included the famous Mesopotamian epics of the Creation, the Flood, and Gilgamesh, many folk tales, fables, proverbs, prayers and omen texts.

Source: *Encyclopaedia Britannica*

PUBLISHER: Margaret Obank

EDITOR: Samuel Shimon

CONTRIBUTING EDITORS
Fadhil al-Azzawi, Issa J Boullata, Peter Clark, Raphael Cohen, Bassam Frangieh, Camilo Gómez-Rivas, Marilyn Hacker, William M Hutchins, Adil Babikir, Imad Khachan, Khaled Mattawa, Anton Shammas, Paul Starkey, Mona Zaki

CONSULTING EDITORS
Etel Adnan, Roger Allen, Mohammed Bennis, Isabella Camera d'Afflitto, Humphrey Davies, Hartmut Fähndrich, Herbert Mason, Saif al-Rahbi, Naomi Shihab Nye, Yasir Suleiman, Susannah Tarbush, Stephen Watts

EDITORIAL ASSISTANTS: Annamaria Basile, Yen-Yen Lu, Maureen O'Rourke, Clare Roberts

ADDITIONAL TRANSLATIONS: Adil Babikir, John Peate

COVER ARTIST: Toufic Abdul-Al

LAYOUT: Banipal Publishing

WEBSITE: www.banipal.co.uk

EDITOR: editor@banipal.co.uk

PUBLISHER: margaret@banipal.co.uk

INQUIRIES: info@banipal.co.uk

SUBSCRIPTIONS: subscribe@banipal.co.uk

ADDRESS: 1 Gough Square, London EC4A 3DE

PRINTED BY Short Run Press Ltd
Bittern Road, Sowton Ind. Est. EXETER EX2 7LW

Photographs not accredited have been donated, photographers unknown.

BANIPAL, ISSN 1461-5363, is published three times a year by Banipal Publishing, 1 Gough Square, London EC4A 3DE

Supported using public funding by
ARTS COUNCIL ENGLAND
LOTTERY FUNDED

Flemish Literature Fund

www.banipal.co.uk

Nouri al-Jarrah

Rasha Omran

Mohamad Alaaedin Abdul Moula

Rosa Yassin Hassan

Khaled Khalifa

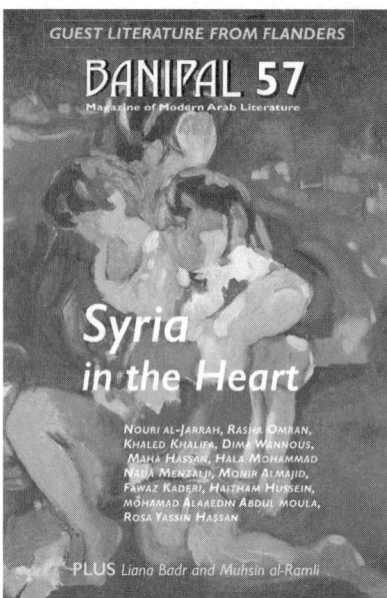

GUEST LITERATURE FROM FLANDERS

BANIPAL 57
Magazine of Modern Arab Literature

Syria in the Heart

NOURI AL-JARRAH, RASHA OMRAN,
KHALED KHALIFA, DIMA WANNOUS,
MAHA HASSAN, HALA MOHAMMAD
NADA MENZALJI, MONIR ALMAJID,
FAWAZ KADERI, HAITHAM HUSSEIN,
MOHAMAD ALAAEDIN ABDUL MOULA,
ROSA YASSIN HASSAN

PLUS Liana Badr and Muhsin al-Ramli

Cover painting by Toufic Abdul-Al

Liana Badr

Muhsin al-Ramli

Charlotte Van den Broeck

Roderik Six

Kathleen Vereecken

Toufic Abdul-Al (1938–2002) is remembered as a major Palestinian artist, born in Acre, forced to leave for Lebanon in 1948, who painted, in oils and water colours, sculpted and drew all his life. We thank his son Tarek for kind permission to reproduce Toufic's painting of a mother holding her children to her, made following the horrific Tel al-Zaatar massacre of 1976.

EDITORIAL – MARGARET OBANK

The last issue of this year (it's such a shame we don't have more in a year!) derives its focus from what is on my mind every day, that is, the disastrous war in Syria. The human capacity to levy war and destruction, inflict medieval torture, foment fear and hatred – annihilation of entire communities if at all possible – is, for me, quite impossible to comprehend. And as publisher of a literary magazine, how to respond to it?

It's such a cliché to say, just after Bob Dylan's Nobel Literature Laureateship, that "The times they are a changin", but there certainly has been over recent years a cataclysmic and generational shift in power relations around the world that has brought continuous war and religious extremism to the heart of the Arab world's oldest civilisations.

Banipal's core mission is to bring readers gems, in translation, from the wealth of creative writing being produced across the Arab world today. **Banipal 57 – Syria in the Heart** brings you twelve Syrian authors, and in addition, two from Palestine and Iraq. The focus on Arab literary modernism and its pioneers has been postponed on account of this most urgent subject of the future of Syria.

While many of us are feeling the acute pain and anguish of watching and experiencing the destruction of Syria, and are often numbed by the relentlessly gruesome and wanton killings and bombings, many of the country's authors are writing, recording and creating a new understanding of, even new relationships with, what is and was their home, their country. In what is a serendipitous coincidence, the twelve authors in **Syria in the Heart** are split equally between female and male fiction writers and female and male poets – three or six of each.

Contemplation and compassion are the key words that I would offer as the unifying force in these texts of Syrian fiction and poetry, translated from a range of authors, all but one of whom are living outside the land mass of destroyed Syria, some for many years, others since the onset of this raging civil war. But where they are now is of no consequence. We are all citizens of the world, but still hold forever in our hearts precious ties, unique experiences, yet to be told histories, haunting memories. The lyrical power of literature is such that in these terrible times it can synthesise all these, meld and consider them, and renew hope in the human condition. These twelve authors have very individual stories and all project their universality.

The protagonist of **Dima Wannous**'s novel *The Frightened* fears fear itself: the novel takes on that question of "the very fear of fear" that "has permeated the souls of most Syrians for many decades". Poet **Rasha Omran**, who ran the Al-Sindyan Cultural Festival until the civil war forced its close and her escape, writes what at first glance is a balladic prose poem, but it erupts with fine touches of surrealism, in recording minutiae of daily life with bursts of grandeur ... "Women poets are like solitary cats ... are mad ... are dreamers ... are crafty ..."

The chapter from **Khaled Khalifa**'s latest novel, *Death is Hard Work*, opens with son Belbol trying to deal with his father's death wish that his bones should "rest in his home village", and finding himself up against checkpoints while becoming anxious about how how death was outlasting the living and how people thought about themselves as "pre-dead".

Poet and film-maker **Hala Mohammad** writes eloquently about the changes that happen after leaving a house and neighbourhood, and how memories "do not a country make". The sorrow and grief at all that's being lost in this war is encapsulated in the lines "*I want to remain suspended in this space / the space that empties my mind of thought / turns my mind into a heart*".

The new novel of **Maha Hassan**, who has lived in France for a number of years, is *Aleppo Metro*, a narrative about displacement, Syria's fleeing and destroyed people and the "savage war", inspired by her own dreams and then nightmares as Aleppo daily burns. Poet **Fawaz Kaderi** mourns the "still, unresponsive" child whose mouth was "full of shouts", while **Nada Menzalji**, also a poet, does not accept the destruction – the house was wrecked but "the scene remained intact".

Haitham Hussein's novel *Hostages of Memory* relates in fascinating detail the story of a Kurdish family moving from village to village in 1960s Syria struggling with extreme poverty to find a life. Back in present-day war-torn Syria is **Rosa Yassin Hassan**'s novel *People under a Spell*, whose characters span the spectrum of opinion and factions, struggling to understand the "rising waves of extremism, hatred and violence"and how it was that Syrian society "collapsed almost completely in such a short period".

Nouri al-Jarrah's poem "Boat to Lesbos" is a dramatic elegy unfurling into the 21st century, through a feast of vivid present-day and historical images and a Greek chorus of spoken voice, the ancient mythology of the constellations. An elegy to all those who have been forced to flee Syria by sea, a particularly poignant line reads "*Nothing is left of Cadmus fleeing with his sister from Tyre in flames but shards on a boat*".

Monir Almajid takes the reader into the heart of Qamishli as a Syrian Kurd growing up in what was then a city of many ethnicities, religions and languages, and is followed by the final author of **Syria in the Heart**, poet **Mohamad Alaaedin Abdul Moula**. His poems are perhaps a fitting conclusion to the feature as they range from language and dreams, to pain and fear, to a photo not yet taken, and to the cemetery watchman who reads "Here lies Syria" on a gravestone.

This year's Frankfurt Book Fair honoured writing in Dutch language from Europe's Flanders and the Netherlands. We, too, are honoured to present, in collaboration with the **Flemish Literature Fund, Guest Literature from Flanders**, featuring six Flemish authors. The introduction gives much food for thought to those involved and interested in developing cultural dialogue through literature. Belgium is a tri-lingual country, with French, Dutch and German the official languages. Belgians can use whichever language they want to – language freedom is embedded in the constitution. Tolerance and acceptance of difference are seen in action, and with all the complexities of sharing and not sharing, of similarity and difference. And now the influx of migrants and refugees there is seeing growing numbers of writers of other languages, such as Arabic, Kurdish and Russian. What struck me about all six authors is that they are unafraid to experiment with both style and content, and offer surprises and inspiration that put the reader on the spot and demand attention.

The successful first annual lecture of the **Saif Ghobash Banipal Prize** to mark ten years of awards for great contemporary Arabic literature translated into English took place at the British Library in October. Anton Shammas enthralled the audience with his lecture entitled *Blind Spots: A millennium of Arabic in translation – from Ibn Al-Haytham to William Faulkner via Don Quixote*, which raised fascinating questions concerning the science of perception, and linguistic and cultural presuppositions over the centuries that have fed into the western cultural canon.

In this issue I am proud to announce a wonderful new collaboration between **Banipal and St Aidan's College, University of Durham,** with the enthusiastic support of the British Council. St Aidan's College and Banipal are establishing an annual **Banipal Visiting Writer Fellowship** for a published author writing in Arabic. The author Fadia Faqir, who is a Fellow of St Aidan's, and I, have been working on this since April this year; now all is ready for the first three-month Fellowship to take place from 23 January 2017. See page 4 above for all details of how to apply.

We open the issue with a finely crafted, poetic short story by the well-known Palestinian author **Liana Badr**, and an excerpt from a powerful novel to be published in translation next year – *The President's Gardens* by Iraqi author **Muhsin al-Ramli**. We end the issue with many book reviews. Enjoy and ponder!

LIANA BADR

One Sky

A SHORT STORY

TRANSLATED BY BECKI MADDOCK

He was standing at the side of the road, atop a pile of gravel, between the asphalt and the rocky mountainside. Frozen in place, with a fixed gaze, like a wax doll, his black eye gleaming at me. His serious stance, like a miniature knight on a chess board, caught my eye. I bent over and picked him up as if he were a piece of carbonised sand. His other eye appeared to be closed. The eyelid was swollen, covering it. Between his eyes was a red scar, evidence of a blow, below which his feathers had been plucked out.

His injury suggested that a predator had pecked him between his eyes but had not succeeded in killing him. One of our group speculated that a passing car had hit the reckless bird, being able to avoid it, as birds do not recognise potential danger posed by moving vehicles. Another commented that a bird of prey must have attacked him to inflict such a severe injury.

I picked him up immediately and wrapped him in the white, silky shawl that still retained a blue mark in the form of the gold brooch that fastens the fabric of the traditional Tunisian sefseri cloak. I thanked God that the changeable spring weather had compelled me to bring what I had wrapped around my neck, so that I could use it to lift the injured bird from the dust without causing it to panic.

Cradling the small bird, I resumed walking towards the grassy slope, above which a patch of blue sky appeared. I hugged him close to my chest, hoping that the beating of my heart would transmit some warmth into his tiny, exhausted body. It seemed to me that the bird's fragility in the face of the random blows was at odds with the strength of his wings that carried him above the laws of earthly gravity. How much stronger than us he was, and yet immeasurably more fragile!

We carried on towards the slope. Above us shone the fresh spring sky, the brightness of which we had not known since the cold days of winter.

We proceed at a vigorous pace, leaving behind us a temporary construction for the curfew, following a month and a half of confinement by the tanks and armoured vehicles that had devastated the city. The soles of our feet enjoy the feel of the solid earth despite the large amount of gravel scattered on it. The features of our faces relax, after having stiffened from compulsory listening to the babble of the political programmes on the satellite television stations, which discuss our situation in a style no different to the entertainment programmes.

Our senses are shaken by the noise of the loudspeakers fixed to the Israeli Jeeps, which multiply around us like dangerous viruses as they recite their orders at us. We walk with all our determination, escaping, albeit temporarily, from the smells of poisonous gas bombs, and the garbage and waste, which has not been collected because of the curfew. Attempting to flee, if only for a moment, from our houses that have become our prisons. Expending most of our energy through our steps placed in the direction of the open air, so that we might forget how many incessant announcements are repeated around us at all hours of the night or day. Trying to ensure that, despite everything, our fundamental dreams of a different life are not shaken from our souls. As if that excursion of ours were no more than a break from all the instructions and orders that have been instilled in us and imposed upon us, like cages of chain mail.

Merely perhaps . . . in order that we peek out between the solid bars of our prison, between one prohibition and another, at another blue patch of the sky of Palestine.

A sky that looks down on mountainous lands encircled by the ancient dry-stone walls that have prevented the earth from crumbling and collapsing since the times of the Romans and Phoenicians. A vast expanse, and over its hills spread the stone huts, like miniature fortresses, their rough stones forming houses to protect the crops and sheep of farmers since times long past, and forgotten by subsequent generations.

Under the shadows of the clouds, ceaselessly wandering above the eternally recurring summits, emerge from time to time the fortifications of Israeli military positions surrounded by barbed wire, ready to assume their roles in the conversion of our agricultural land into colonial settlements.

Looking from the West, these occupation positions surrounded by searchlights and barbed wire, with their immoral nature, are bathed in the splendour transmitted by these hills over which advance infinite clusters of olive trees. Converging in turn with the streamlined peaks stretching to the distant sea. Above its bright, shimmering waters another sky gently touches that iridescent, red copper twilight of the evening.

A sea, whose shimmering shadows we only glimpse from afar, because it remains hidden in the direction of the beach, which we are forbidden from reaching. Yet we never tire of gazing towards it whenever possible, making walking to it evidence of nostalgia. We use as a pretext the search for the flowers which the desert bears at this time of year. Scarlet anemones and rosy-lilac gazelles' horns, or yellow aspalathus. We search for various types of small lilies, with rippling, rose-like sheen, our tense gazes like closed petals, bursting towards their ripeness, as if we are redrawing the freedom of release from the closed borders imposed upon us.

We complete our tour, and the small bird with the closed eye is wrapped in the shawl against my chest, and we took him along with us.

At home, I named him Robin, based on the assurances of our bird-loving neighbour. When I expressed my doubt about the name due to the incomplete red ruff on his neck feathers, he told me: "This is a young bird. The full red has not yet appeared on his feathers."

At home, I put him under a sieve made of metal wire and left him some water and seeds. The first day passed and he was rigid and motionless. He stood frozen, as if he had been glued in place. He could not be seen clearly between the thin metal wires, as his dark colouring blended with the metal. He was unmoving and did not budge. I recalled the day a canary froze in my house, when his cage accidentally fell from the window ledge while I was out. The shock had caused it to stand frozen in place for two days without eating or drinking. Thus, I assessed that Robin would get better after a day or two.

It seemed to me then that however small birds are they have expressions and we can understand how they feel from their appearance. Movement is a sign of happiness. I put down some seeds and water for him and at night I felt pleased because he was in a safe place. He did not move the next day either, but a few seeds were missing from the handful that I had put in the dish.

I had to wait, listening to the Israeli loudspeakers circulating with the Jeeps for three more days until they announced the lifting of the curfew. During that time Robin did not move and he did not make a sound. There was nothing to indicate that he was getting better except his closed eye, which began to open little by little, although it remained smaller than his main, healthy eye.

I asked our neighbour, the bird breeder, whether I should keep him or release him. He assured me that Robin was a wild bird and could not endure captivity if he lived in a cage inside the house and that the best thing was definitely to return him to the wild as soon as possible before he became depressed and stopped eating and drinking.

I tossed and turned for a long time in bed, lying, as I did every night, in an impromptu position, in fear of the thundering clashes during the night. I battled unsuccessfully that premature, early-morning wakefulness that embitters my day, like the punishment of prisons. For no matter how securely the windows are closed, the reverberation of the loudspeakers penetrates the walls bringing us the voice of the Israeli officer, who in his poor, grammatically incorrect Arabic, filled with linguistic errors, orders us to stay in our houses that day, or informs us of the required time we must return home in the event that the curfew is lifted for a few hours.

It was an unpleasant morning, its disquiet relieved only by my preparations for the pleasing idea of returning Robin to his original habitat, to that spot where we had walked on that radiant day.

I did not have enough time because the curfew would soon be lifted and I had to return him to his original place, then go to stand in the long queue at the bakery, and afterwards scour the few shops for some vegetables.

My friend and I went by car to the western side of the city. In my hands was the metal sieve, which covered the dish in which Robin stood. The place was not beautiful, as we had thought it last time. There was a housing development occupying its edges turning it into a pit with newly-built flats multiplying in it, lined up in haphazard, random rows, with scrap metal, piles of earth and building materials in front of them.

We looked for a tree near where we had found him but were unsuccessful. We found only a small pine tree that had been accidentally left behind, far from the excavations of the building sites. We walked over the small rocks, and the snatching thorns, and homes of wild brambles, their thorns tugging at our clothes, until we reached that tree, standing at almost the highest point among the hills.

The tree did not look like a safe refuge but there was no alternative except the low thorns entwined around the rocks. Robin would surely know how to handle himself because a few days in the house would not be enough to eliminate his wild instinct. I approached the tree and placed him on one of its short branches. To my great surprise, he fell to the ground and did not hold onto the branch. I rushed to him, picked him up, and placed him on another branch of the tree. It seemed as if there was some impediment to his attachment to the place, because he was falling off the tree immediately. Perhaps he was still suffering from dizziness and loss of balance!

Nevertheless, there was no alternative. So I ran after him when he flew at a low altitude, immediately afterwards falling near a smooth rock, and I picked him up again so as to put him back on the tree branch. He restrained himself a little this time but it was not long before he lost his balance and fell once more.

There was no possibility of giving up, and time was running out. I had to return with my friend before it became dangerously late. He showed a little improvement at keeping his balance, trying to fly again each time. I could not take him back with me, and he had to hurry up and fly before he was finished off by the cats in the neighbouring residential district.

The seventh time he flew several metres horizontally then fell.

And the eighth . . . and after more than ten attempts, he flew.

He flew.

Not high enough, but enough to take him away from that place and towards another.

He flew! And he disappeared!

And I have not seen him again since that moment.

Not long after his departure, at the end of that spring, I was again walking in that area when I noticed something that I had always seen before but that had not entered my field of vision. One of the birds of prey was circling high above like a helicopter. Staring, searching for prey, that might be a small bird like Robin. After that I began to realise that that bird was spending his days constantly circling there above the high mountain, directly above that small tree.

A high mountain, under a blue sky looking down on hills and ancient olive trees, and mountains overlooking a captivating sea, invaded by colonising settlements advancing from the histories of ancient wars. Vines still encircle the ruins of the farmers' stone huts of long ago, and beside the sea nestle cities, whose inhabitants have left and others have taken over, after wars that have continued for decades.

All that under one sky!

Is that why Robin flew far away and I have not seen him again since that moment?

Translated from the author's collection *Sama'a Waahida* (One Sky), published by Saqi Books, 2007

MUHSIN AL-RAMLI

Sons of the Earth Crack

CHAPTER I FROM THE NOVEL

THE PRESIDENT'S GARDENS

TRANSLATED BY LUKE LEAFGREN

In a land without bananas, the village awoke to nine banana crates, each containing the severed head of one of its sons. Along with each head was an I.D. card to identify the victim since some of the faces were completely disfigured, either by torture before the beheading or by something similar after the slaughter. The characteristic features by which they had been known through all the years of their bygone lives were no longer present to distinguish them.

The first person to notice these crates alongside the main street was the dull-witted herdsman, Isma'il. Curious, he approached without dismounting from his donkey. The donkey's image was inextricably tied to Isma'il's in the minds of the people because of how long he had ridden it – sidesaddle, both legs hanging down on the same side – as though the two of them shared one body. As soon as Isma'il saw the bloody heads inside the boxes, he slid off his donkey and bent close, poking at them with the end of his staff. He recognised some of the heads. All traces of sleep fled his eyes as he rubbed them to make sure he wasn't dreaming. Then he looked around to confirm he was in his own village and not somewhere else.

The last silver light of dawn was filling the street. The shops on either side were closed. The sleeping village was calm and still, apart from the crowing of a rooster and the barking of a distant dog, responding to another dog in some yet more distant corner. In that moment, Isma'il felt liberated from the ancient sense of guilt that had pursued him in nightmares ever since, as a boy, he cut out the

tongue of a goat that had annoyed him with its bleating when he was braiding a wool belt for Hamida amid the solitary silence of Hyena Valley.

In that same moment, Isma'il's tongue recovered from its paralysis, and he began screaming at the top of his lungs, causing his donkey to jump, his flock of sheep to freeze, and the pigeons and sparrows to launch from the treetops and rooftops. He kept yelling without realising what he was saying, and his cries seemed to resemble the bleating of that goat whose tongue he had cut out and grilled. He kept yelling until he saw people rushing towards him from some of the village houses – then all the people from all the houses, after the alarm was raised over the mosque's loudspeakers.

And if Abdullah Kafka had spoken about this incident, he would have said, "It was on the third day of the month of Ramadan, 2006. According to ancient history, that was when a strange amorphous blob with a giant body and a small head, called America, came from across the oceans and occupied a country named Iraq. Historians make clear in some footnotes that the people of that time had hearts that were primitive in their cruelty, savage hearts, like beasts of prey. As a result, among the injurious relations they had with each other were such dishonourable deeds as assault, terrorism, wars, invasions, and occupations. In those remote times, the heart of humanity was sunk in darkness. It wasn't a darkness of intellect or vision, such that man was unable to cogitate upon the murder of his brother man. Rather, it was much worse, in that he might actually follow through with it."

This is how Abdullah Kafka would see and speak about everything that happened, describing it all as ancient, lost, dead history. The present and the future did not exist at all for him. There was only the past, and all of it was black. Some of it died irrevocably and did not return, and the rest of it was repeated later, in a time that other people called the future.

So for all the years since his return from captivity in Iran, Abdullah Kafka, that prince of pessimists, had been content to sit at the same seat in the corner of the village café from the moment it opened its doors in the morning until it closed after midnight. Sipping cups of bitter coffee and glasses of tea black as ink, he would smoke a nargileh absent-mindedly or just listen in silence. He returned greetings with a nod of his head or a gesture with a hand that still gripped the smoking nozzle of the water pipe. If he spoke, or rather, if he was forced to speak, he would go on speaking interminably, or he would be satisfied with a comment of no more than a few words.

So it was one spring when they informed him that the river had flooded. It overflowed its banks and covered the fields and gardens, carrying off the nearby huts and mud houses and unearthing the hillside cemetery to scatter the bones and skulls of the dearly departed. Abdullah Kafka did not say a thing. Ignoring the alarm of those bringing the news, he continued puffing on his water pipe as people ran in every direction before him. He said nothing until Isma'il the herdsman came in, petrified and howling, because the flood had swept away his animal pen and carried off ten sheep and one of his goats. He was sobbing as he described how his goat had floated on the surface of the water, brown with flotsam and mud. It was bleating and looking at him, as though in supplication, and Isma'il could do nothing to save it because he did not know how to swim.

Isma'il's despair filled the café: "The water is rising. It's creeping towards the rest of the village! It's the end! It's the Day of Judgment and the end of the world!"

At this, Abdullah Kafka cleared his throat and asked him calmly, "And did the water rise so much that your goat's back touched the sky above us?"

"No," Isma'il said.

Abdullah said to him, "Then this is nothing. But would that the end had come and brought the heavens down to the earth." And he turned deliberately back to his pipe and went on smoking.

As for this morning, when they informed him that the head of his lifelong companion Ibrahim was among the nine, Abdullah replied, "It is finished! He has attained his rest. For this time he has truly died, leaving us to the chaos of fate and the futility of waiting for our own deaths, we the living dead."

Abdullah fell silent and remained motionless apart from the rise and fall of his chest with each breath. He sat frozen there for several moments. Then he began to smoke and smoke. And for the first time, the people saw tears stream from his unblinking eyes. He did not wipe them away, and he did not stop smoking.

When the news reached the third member of their lifelong brotherhood, Sheikh Tariq, he felt faint and nearly collapsed. He sat down quickly, propping up his spirit — so as not to kill himself — by reciting the many religious sayings he had learned by heart and which were always on the tip of his tongue. He wept and asked God's forgiveness; he wept and cursed the devil so as not to be driven to despair; he wept and wept until the tears wet the edges of his red, henna-dyed beard.

Questions from the onlookers saved Tariq from succumbing to an even longer bout of sobbing. "What do we do, O sheikh? Do we bury the heads on their own, or do we wait until we come upon their bodies and bury them together? They were killed in Baghdad, or on the road to Baghdad, and now Baghdad is a chaos choking on anonymous corpses, buried explosives, car bombs, foreigners, and deceit. It might be impossible to find their bodies."

Tariq said, "It's best to bury the heads, and if their bodies are discovered later on, it's not a problem for them to be buried with the heads, or separately, or in the place where they are found. Our sons and brothers are not more venerable or better than the prince of martyrs, Hussein, grandson of the Prophet, whose head they buried in Egypt or Syria while his body stayed in Iraq. Make haste to bury the heads, for the way to honour the dead is to bury them."

Only Qisma, the widow who became an orphan that early morning, opposed them and wanted to keep the head of her father Ibrahim unburied until his body was found. But she resisted in vain when the men refused and rebuked her, saying, "Hold your tongue, woman, and cease this madness! What do you know about such things?"

They pushed her away to where the women were gathered, many of whom were surprised at Qisma's stance since they knew she had not always seen eye to eye with her father. Nevertheless, as was her wont, Qisma refused to give in and began planning her next steps. Only her fat neighbour Amira supported her and wanted to do the same thing, to preserve her husband's head in the freezer until they located his body.

Each head had a story. Every one of these nine heads had a family and dreams and the horror of being slaughtered, just like the hundreds of thousands slain in a country stained with blood since its founding and until God inherits the earth and everyone on it. And if every victim had a book, Iraq in its entirety would become a huge library, impossible ever to catalogue.

Sheikh Tariq said, "Do not wash the heads, for they are martyrs. A martyr is not washed before being buried because he is purified just as he is. His wounds will exude the scent of musk on the Day of Resurrection."

As the last rites were being performed for the heads, Tariq approached the head of Ibrahim and fell upon it, hugging it to his chest and kissing it so hard that his embrace scraped away the scabs formed by dirt and congealed blood that stopped up the wounds and the veins in the neck. The blood drained from it afresh and stained the front of the sheikh's white robe, his hands, and his beard. They gently pulled him away and wrapped the head in a white burial shroud to match the others, which they buried together in a line. In the end, they dug complete graves the length of a normal man, not the size of children's, even though they lowered only the heads into their depths.

Abdullah Kafka did not attend the funeral but stayed at the café, smoking. No-one blamed him, even though all the people of the village knew the strength of the bond that had existed between these three men since childhood, such that they were called by various epithets, all of which played on the idea of three – "the eternal triad", "the happy threesome", or even "the three butt cheeks in the same briefs" and "the triple balls" and so on – because they would almost never be seen apart from each other until destiny separated them in the days of the Iraq–Iran War. But the most widely used name was "sons of the earth crack". That name had a story, which was itself a testament to the strength of their early alliance.

It went back to the early years of their boyhood, the days when they would swim in the Tigris during the burning heat of July afternoons, quarrel with the girls bathing and washing clothes near the shore, hunt at night for the sand grouse sleeping in the nearby deserts, root out snakes and jerboa from their holes to break off their teeth, and drive off the wolves and jackals. When the Bedouin herdsman Jad'an spotted them near his tent, he did not recognise them, even though he knew nearly all the villagers on account of his living there with his family and his flock of sheep for one month each year, right after the harvest. He asked Abdullah, "Whose son are you?" And because Abdullah did not know his real father, he was quiet for a moment and then said, "I'm the son of the earth crack." Jad'an turned to Ibrahim and Tariq with the same question, and they gave the same answer out of solidarity with Abdullah. At that, the Bedouin fell silent for a while, stroking his beard as if in thought, and said,

"Yes, we are all sons of the earth crack. The earth is our mother, all of us. Out of her we are born, and to her we return."

Jad'an mussed their hair affectionately and invited them to his tent to taste "the best butter in the world", as he called it, which was the butter of his wife, Umm Fahda, and to drink some of the milk from her village. The invitation pleased them to the same degree as it filled their souls with fear and trembling, for this was an unexpected opportunity for Tariq to see Fahda, daughter of Jad'an and Umm Fahda, inside her tent, instead of making secret rendezvous with her between the sacks of harvested wheat and barley or among the flock of resting ewes. Did her father know what had been going on between them, and was his invitation nothing more than an ambush to trap them and do to them God knows what? Stories of Bedouin cruelty and betrayals were notorious, especially when connected to questions of honour.

Jad'an later told the story to the village elders as they sat together, drinking their morning coffee. They all burst out laughing and praised the boys' solidarity and fidelity to the ideal of true friendship. The story circulated widely, just as everything said in the village reached every ear, even when whispered in confidence. From that time the name "sons of the earth crack" became commonplace.

Abdullah wasn't lying when he said that he was the son of the earth crack, for that is what he knew at the time, as did everyone else. But now, nearly fifty years old, he was the only one who knew the origin of the story. The mayor's wife, who had tarried in life until he returned from the long years of his captivity in Iran, had told him the truth of the matter.

He alone knew that she was his grandmother, and that the dull-witted herdsman Isma'il was his maternal uncle. His story was like something out of the old melodramas from India, so it was no surprise that he was known for defining life as "a Hindi movie".

About himself he would say, "I am a victim and the son of victims. I am the son of the murdered going back to Abel, and I'm surprised not to have been killed yet." Then he would add, "The logic of my ancestors' history stipulates that my death be connected with love. Perhaps my failure to bind myself to the one I loved is what has come between me and my death. Or else that failure itself is my true downfall . . . Perhaps I am the final sentence in this volume containing the family tree of the murdered."

Abdullah did not clarify to anyone the true secret behind his allusions. And no-one asked him for any explanation since they were used to such pronouncements, which they called his "philosophising". The inscrutability of these sayings usually baffled them, and people would interpret them as they pleased or else forget about them entirely. Abdullah did not disclose the secret even to his lifelong friends despite their implicit mutual pledge to secrecy. In turn, they too carried secrets in their breasts that they resolved would remain confined unto death. Everybody has a secret, maybe more than one, which they decide not to reveal to anyone. Sometimes because it is shameful, embarrassing, or painful. Sometimes because they do not find the right opportunity to announce it: the secret's time hasn't come, or else it has passed, and its revelation no longer carries any meaning or importance.

Abdullah was raised at the hands of good parents who loved him as though he were the fruit of their loins. If he had been a girl, they would have named him Hadiya, "gift", because they believed he was "a gift from above". Abdullah's parents said that repeatedly throughout their lives.

Salih and Maryam's small mud house was at the very edge of the village, on the side of the hill by the river. One spring dawn, when the white of the first approaching light scattered the last remnants of the retreating darkness, Maryam awoke as usual and went out to the square mud stall that rose as high as the shoulder of someone standing beside it. At a distance of sixty steps from the door, it was situated in the furthest part of the dwelling's courtyard, right above a deep crack in the side of the hill. This crack had been made by a torrential rain many long years before, and Salih had put it to good use as a toilet, which they called "the pit".

Previously, Salih and Maryam, like everyone living on the outskirts of the village, used to do their business in the river valley, the thickets, or out in the open after nightfall. With the crack, Salih did nothing more than construct the mud wall, and since it cost him nothing, he chalked it up to his own ingenuity. You only had to spread your legs to either side of the crack and squat down, then expel your excretions into the mouth of the dark opening, waiting to hear the sound of its fall, hidden in the depths far below.

Some suggested this crack was an old well, reopened by the rain. Others said that perhaps the hill contained ancient ruins, for when digging wells or kneading mud to build their houses or make a bread oven, people often found urns, bracelets, earrings, tablets, belts, swords, and armour made from brass, gold, and silver. They would give anything made for women as gifts to their own wives and keep anything made for men as ornaments to put on the walls of their reception rooms. They used the urns – after pouring out the bones and washing them – to cool water or pickle vegetables. As for the ceramic tablets, which had drawings and inscriptions scratched upon them, these they used as doorsteps, or to reinforce door frames, or as part of a window, or under the legs of beds or wardrobes to fix their balance.

That morning, before Maryam went into "the pit", she saw a bundle of cloth propped up against the wall next to the entrance, near the outer opening of the crack. She was startled and put her hand to her mouth, then to her breast. As she calmed down and took a deep breath, she reached her hand out cautiously to the top of the bundle and slowly drew back the edges of the cloth. She was terrified to see the face of a suckling babe, asleep. She ran back to the house and shook Salih until the entire bed shook with him. He woke up and asked what the matter was. Maryam stuttered as she pointed outside, "A baby – a baby – the pit – a baby!" And if it were not the case that Salih had never before seen his wife in such a state of bewilderment, he would not have hurried out barefoot and in his pyjamas.

They carried the bundle inside and set it down. They kept looking at each other in silence, their unspoken thoughts hanging in the air. "Salih," Maryam said at last, "do you think it is a gift from God in return for our patience? Is it an answer to our prayers?"

He said, "I don't know. But what could have brought it here? I'll go to dawn prayers at the mosque and ask if anyone has lost a baby."

He got up and headed out to "the pit" in order to perform the ritual purification. He walked around the structure twice as though looking for something – perhaps another baby. He squatted inside and strained but only gas came out. He washed and went back to put on his clean robe. He stared at the face of the child and said, "Please check – is it a boy or a girl?"

Maryam uncovered the infant with trembling fingers and burst into tears. "It's a boy!"

Salih went out as though a wind were at his back – and a second wind pulling him from the front. As soon as he arrived at the mosque, he told Sheikh Zahir, the imam, what had happened so that he could inform the congregation. Contrary to Salih's expectations, Zahir wasn't surprised, a response Salih put down to the sheikh's sophistication, the breadth of his knowledge, his equanimity, and the firmness of his faith.

After the prayers, the imam addressed the people, asking them about the matter. Given that no-one there had lost a baby or heard about anyone losing a baby, Zahir said, "Let those who are present inform those who are absent. Tell all the people of the village. And if no-one claims the child and establishes his paternity within three days, then the infant belongs to Salih and Maryam. It is undoubtedly a gift from the Lord of creation for their patience, their goodness, and their faith."

Everyone agreed, and indeed, it warmed their hearts on account of their affection for Salih. At first they hoped, then they said, and in the end they believed that the matter truly was a miracle, God's recompense to the good and patient couple.

Salih's face couldn't hide the tears gleaming in his eyes. And as

soon as he got outside, he hurried home, carried along by the same gale at his back. Beaming, he came in to where Maryam was waiting and said, "It really is a gift, Maryam, just as you said! And if it had been a girl, we would have named her that, 'Hadiya'. But now, we'll name him . . . we'll name him Abdullah, after my father, who died dreaming of a grandson to carry his name."

Maryam was about to trill with joy, but Salih stopped her, even though the force of his own exultation would have made him trill had he known how. "Not now," he said. "Wait another two days, and at that time we'll slaughter our bull and hold a huge feast for everyone. A party with dancing, just like a wedding. Then you can trill all you want."

And so it was.

THE PRESIDENT'S GARDENS

On the third day of Ramadan, the village wakes to find the severed heads of nine of its sons stacked in banana crates by the bus stop. One of them belonged to one of the most wanted men in Iraq, known to his friends as Ibrahim the Fated. How did this good and humble man earn the enmity of so many? What did he do to deserve such a death? The answer lies in his lifelong friendship with Abdullah Kafka and Tariq the Befuddled, who each have their own remarkable stories to tell. It lies on the scarred, irradiated battlefields of the Gulf War and in the ashes of a revolution strangled in its cradle. It lies in the steadfast love of his wife and the festering scorn of his daughter. And, above all, it lies behind the locked gates of The President's Gardens, buried alongside the countless victims of a pitiless reign of terror.

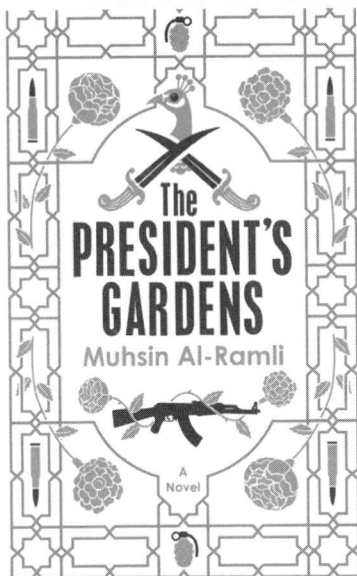

The President's Garden is published by Maclehose Press, 20 April 2017, paperback (ISBN: 9780857056788), £12.00; Ebook (ISBN: 9780857056795).

For more information, see https://www.quercusbooks.co.uk/books/detail.page?isbn=9780857056788

Syria in the heart

Dima Wannous

Rasha Omran

Khaled Khalifa

Hala Mohammad

Maha Hassan

Fawaz Kaderi

Haitham Hussein

Rosa Yassin Hassan

Nada Menzalji

Nouri al-Jarrah

Monir Almajid

Mohamad A. A. Moula

DIMA WANNOUS

The Frightened

A CHAPTER FROM THE NOVEL

TRANSLATED BY JULIA IHNATOWICZ

N aseem put the phone down and withdrew into himself. I could hear nothing but silence. I felt at peace. Like someone who had suddenly shut their eyes. And in this case, the shutting wasn't just a physical action. Rather, it was like someone who was closing their eyes, their heart and their soul, so that all the anxiety and all the fear was extinguished and replaced with a feeling of lightness, and of freedom from everything that had been and everything that would be. A freedom from memory. How many times have I dreamt of shaking my head in the wind so that all memory streams out of it and I can relax. How often have I wished to forget who I am, what I'm called, where I was born, who I live with, who I'm friends with, where I've been, in which street exactly I have found myself, who I love; I wished to forget, to lose all of my memory in one go. Because I know that memory either is or isn't. You either reconcile yourself to it, with all the pressures it brings, all the happiness, joy and fear, or you give it up completely, to the point where you forget your own name. I want to forget my name. Forget my name? Really? Or do I want them to forget my name? Am I aching because of myself or because of what others expect of me? I lived for many years convinced that I hated my own self. Then I woke up one day and discovered that I love and esteem her, but what keeps me up at night is other people. Except, in reality, it's only self-longing for who I am. I miss her, my lonely, fragile self, who exists only in her obligations. Why do we tire our souls so that other people's demands can live, and they are at peace and live in peace ? What good is giving other people peacefulness when at the same time we live in terrible fear?

Naseem put down the receiver, withdrawing into himself, and I felt a strange kind of peace. As I got off the bed, a dreadful ache seized my stomach, as if I hadn't savoured a single morsel for days. Really, I don't eat much any more.

I've become a creature against eating. An enemy of eating. I take a piece of bread, as if I were picking up a rock that I would swallow, that would stick in my gullet, making its way to my stomach, choking me and making me tired. I'm no longer brave enough to swallow much. As soon as the food brushes against my stomach I feel tired and fatigued, as if I've eaten a whole sheep. Hunger makes me feel safe. It's as if the emptiness in my belly betrays the emptiness in my head, my memory, and my soul. I like this emptiness. I'm beginning to gallop through it like a lonely little cloud in the wide open sky. The hunger makes me feel light, it frees me from overbearing duties, even the need to digest. Digestion takes a level of effort I can no longer stand. The heart is forced to beat more than usual, the intestines scrunch up and then relax, and the belly makes noises. I got off my bed, enjoying my hunger this time, and knew that despite my great hunger, I wouldn't eat much. I left my room for the living room. My mother is sitting on the red sofa, clutching a book that she started weeks ago. I swear she's been staring at the same page, page 24, for days. My mother, who has become a crumpled little heap beneath a soft blanket on the sofa, reads a sentence, repeats it, and re-reads it. No sooner has she moved on to the next sentence than she discovers she has to re-read the last one, which she's read over and over. She's been gazing at the same sentence, reading it, and re-reading it. I don't know whether she's really been reading for hours, or whether she's staring at it so as not to stare into emptiness. The emptiness increases her sense of madness. She hasn't lost her mind, but she's under the delusion that she has. She tells me she'll get Alzheimer's very soon. I jokingly tell her to hurry up and get on with it. She looks wearily at me and smiles an odd smile, the nature of which I don't understand but I feel a sort of bitterness seeping out of that closed, fleeting smile that lasts only a few seconds. My mother's charm was in her smile. It was she who was good at laughing and making merry, she who is an emaciated pile of a body under a soft blanket. I tell her that Alzheimer's eases the weight of death. It makes us wish for her death rather than waiting for it in fear. It makes us swap obsequies for festivities. It makes us? "Who's "we"?" my mother asks me, and I am silent.

Sitting on the sofa, reading the same page 24 as she has been doing for days, my mother was suddenly old. I haven't grasped how my mother grew old. We went to sleep and she was young, we woke up and like that, she was old. Had she aged over night? Is one night enough? Is a handful of dreams from a single night enough for a person to get as old as this? I say that it's lucky she became old at night and not in the middle of the day, for instance, as I would have been terrified. If, for example, she'd gone into the kitchen to make breakfast and come out a few minutes later and she'd been old. Or if she'd said to me quietly and a bit annoyed: "Sulayma, I'm going to have the bath," and then come out of the bathroom old. It's good luck that my mother aged at night and we woke to find her old. Who's "we"? Just her and me. Even when Fouad disappeared, she didn't age. She cried a lot, but didn't age. Are the tears the reason? Maybe. As my mother says, tears wash the soul. Or maybe tears took the place of ageing. She could either cry or get old. She cried a lot, and fiercely, until her tears dried up, as she tells me over and over again. When her tears dried up, my mother went to sleep a young woman, then woke up old. I haven't told her that I haven't slept since he disappeared. I haven't told her that I wish for his death every evening, every morning, every moment. I pray to God, worshipping and memorising verses from the Qur'an, so that some lord will grant my prayers. I try in vain to put his image out of my mind.

In the first months of his disappearance I thought that shutting my eyes would call his image to my mind, so I didn't shut them. For many nights I resisted closing them, until I was exhausted and fell asleep for a long time. I awoke with renewed energy and kept them open again day and night for a week, and so on. I haven't spoken to my mother, and she hasn't spoken to me. I was sure she was hoping he was dead, too. How could a mother's heart be so calm and cold when her son is alive and being subjected to torture all the time? To soothe my soul, I told myself that a mother's heart is her guide and that my mother could feel that Fouad had departed from this life, and that's how she slept soundly. She must have known, or how could she have gone on all these months? It's true that she grew old all of a sudden over night, but she's sitting quietly now on the sofa reading page 24.

Once, I told Kameel how, when I was young, I used to imagine my parents and only brother being subjected to abuse, or beatings, or torture. I'd imagine them drowning. Not naturally, in the way that Naseem fears, but rather I'd picture some evil people taking pleasure in drowning and torturing them. I used to cry at night, alone in my bed, in the knowledge that they were all fine, tucked up safe in their beds. We examined, Kameel and I, the reasons for these thoughts and ideas. For how could a child of nine or ten, living in a quiet home that lacked neither love nor calm, have such violent thoughts as these? I don't remember Kameel's reaction exactly. But I remember he described what was happening to me as self-flagellation. Yes, I was self-flagellating, and I still am. I see my father down on his knees, kissing someone's boots. Today, I think that person was an officer. But I'm not sure I pictured an officer in my childhood, or whether the idea of an officer was acquired with the passing of an age of similar, but real images. These images are no longer imagined! There's someone kissing an officer's boots every moment now. Is the idea as simple as that? Do you believe it? Don't we say in our conversations that a person dies every moment somewhere in this wide world? Don't we say that there's a woman giving birth every second? And we've also got to the point where we say that there's now a Syrian down on his knees every minute, forced to kiss some officer's boots.

After Fouad disappeared, I blamed myself. What good was spending my childhood self-flagellating? When now I have to do the same thing, for plausible reasons and not just for a fantasy. If I had known. If I had predicted what was going to happen, I wouldn't have spent time on those thoughts at an earlier point. I would have enjoyed peaceful sleep, undisturbed by a sick imagination. Then I consoled myself with my father's death. My father died ten years ago. He didn't die under torture and wasn't subjected to abuse in the way I always used to imagine. My mother says that fear killed him. But I don't believe her. Maybe I don't want to believe her. My father died. He was sixty. He fell asleep and didn't wake up. Just like my mother, who went to sleep and woke up an old woman. He wasn't able to make the leap between the two states, so he fell into death. Perhaps he didn't want to get old, so he preferred to die. In any case, he died and took with him the associated self-flagellation. I no longer imagine him except in all his elegance and delicacy, standing or sitting, not kneeling.

I was five when we left our city for Damascus. I don't remember that time except for a few snippets, which I think aren't from my memory so much as my mother's as she related them. I get lost in my memories of childhood between what I actually remember for myself and what's been recounted either to me or in front of me. My mother tells a story of how my father pissed in his pants and went on to beg her to pack their belongings, take their children, and leave for Damascus. My mother couldn't find the words. My father's brown trousers became dark around the crotch and thighs. My father pissed himself. Today I think about how my mother told us that story one morning after his death. Why did she tell it after he died? Why did she want us to know? Was it to convince us that it was fear that killed him? She also said that he decided to leave their city of Hama, even though he was a doctor! She said it exactly like that. When her sentence finished, an exclamation mark appeared to seal her lips. She raised her eyebrows and shook her head with a sneer. To this day, I don't know if she missed him. I'm beset by the feeling that she was pleased about his death. She never told me that his death made her happy. But I saw it in her body, her soul, and her eyes. She once said something to the effect that fear is draining and exhausting. She said she had lived with him for thirty-two years of fear. When my mother says the number, she bites down on the letters and separates them from one another so we feel the effect of the years, and their weight: "Thirty. Two. Years!" Yes, my father left his city out of fear of the death and destruction he saw in the streets. He fled with his family to Damascus and stayed there until after the massacre had finished and everyone who survived had returned to their homes and their lives. They certainly went back to their homes, but did they really go back to their lives? Was life the same and did it go back to its rhythm as if nothing had happened? Does one who has breathed in the scent of death recover their sense of smell? My father didn't talk, except once, about Hama. He was able to do what I couldn't. He was able to wipe it from his memory. He preserved the memories he wanted.

We lived in the Ain al-Kirsh district of Damascus, and my father rented a clinic in the same building that we lived in. "How can he treat the Damascenes after running away from treating his own people?" This question goes round in my head like an echo of the many times my mother repeated it in front of me. I used to feel sorry for my father. When I imagined the torture parties that he, my mother and Fouad were subjected to, the one that troubled my heart the most was my father. Of them all, he was the most affected by the pain. I see his face contorted in agony. What most overwhelmed me were the begging and imploring words that escaped his injured mouth in the form of tired whispers. I would picture him saying: "For God's sake, kill me. Release me. I can't bear any more." And I would cry. I would long for him at night, so I would steal out of my bed into their room and go to the right side of the bed where my father used to sleep. I stood by his head, stretching out my little finger towards his nose, to reassure myself that he was still alive, despite the bloody torture party. (When I read the manuscript for Naseem's latest novel, I saw myself. Naseem robbed me when he wrote that novel. I haven't told him that.) As for my mother and Fouad, they were also more resilient! Their features didn't plead for pity. On the contrary, they had a bravery and stubbornness. Only my father's appearance captured my soul. Luckily, he died and hasn't been forced to produce his ID at one of the checkpoints and answer embarrassing questions.

Did Kameel make the link between my passion for self-flagellation and the Hama massacre and our move to Damascus? I don't remember but I don't think so. Because I don't know exactly what happened and in Damascus I've lived nothing but a stable life. I remember that a picture of Hafez al-Assad used to hang in my father's clinic. I remember it made my mother extremely angry: "You hang up a picture of the man who killed your people? Does that make you happy? Isn't it enough that you ran away? Do you know who kills the victim and walks in his funeral?" She would ask him this without bothering about his answer. She didn't say, for instance: "It's you who kills the victim and walks in his funeral." Rather, she'd most likely leave him confused and upset at her relentless insistence on his culpability. She'd often add in something close to a whisper: "I don't blame the other Syrians for shutting their doors in our faces." Here, again, she wouldn't say that she couldn't blame them in this case because some of their own people (my father most of all) had run away, leaving his own countrymen to die alone, without treating them or at least standing by them, inhaling the scent of their deaths, gazing on their corpses tossed into the street, the blood flowing out of them. My father, wretched, would reply: "Yes, it's because I'm from Hama I've hung up the picture! Because my sin is so great." He would say this, or something similar, and leave the house to go to the clinic, or the café where he met his friends. In some way, the picture was a confession that he didn't belong to that place. That he had broken his tie and deleted what had happened from his memory, he had forgiven, forgotten and made peace. My father only wanted to live and nurture his little family. So what did my

mother want throughout those long tired years of blaming and relentlessly re-
minding him of his high treason? What did she want other than to foster hatred
in us? Did she wish, for instance, that we had stayed in Hama and that her husband had been killed? Would her husband's death, like the rest of them in
Hama, have helped her to find peace in a memory where her other countrymen
live? Is death, in some cases, a stimulus for life and hatred? Would my mother
have preferred the life of a widow, with all its dignity and bravery, to living
with a "cowardly" and "submissive" husband for "Thirty. Two. Years" – with her
stress and separation between the letters.

I jokingly told Naseem to write my father's story. But he didn't get the joke,
even in the context. Yes, Naseem is serious to the point of tedium. He's not
even good at telling jokes. He tells them in an overly serious way, keeping his
brow furrowed so that the knot between his eyebrows has become a part of
the lines on his face, as if it was born with him, and he with it. A knot has
formed between them and vehemently stayed put, as if it is the point from
which his soul issues, and not from his breast or his mother's womb. As if it is
this knot that expresses his soul. Naseem didn't write my father's story. Nor
could my mother find it in the manuscript of his last novel. But he has stolen

About The Frightened

A novel about fear – not just about fear itself, but the very fear of fear
– cannot be brief. It is something that has permeated the souls of
most Syrians for many decades. It has become part of their very body
tissue; it shapes the very contours of their temperament. It is a fear I lived
with – on the street, in school – as one of the "Ba'athist vanguard" generation,
the "revolutionary youth" of a regime-manufactured revolution encompassing
every form of injustice, oppression, intimidation, pacification and subjugation
the mind can sense of that brutality in whose shadow I spent my whole childhood. I turned into a creature bodily estranged from all others; one's body
becomes all that belongs to the space and time that one is forced to live in.

Naseem – one among 23 million other Syrians – fears fear itself; he avoids
or runs away from it as much as he can and whenever he can. He is just one of
many millions living alien, brutal lives in a nation regulated by terror, suspicion,
and a self-belief diminished to the point of almost vanishing, of almost ceasing

mine. I haven't told him that. Even if I did, he would absolutely deny it. He'd say that the story of his novel's heroine doesn't converge with my story in any shape or form. And I'd get confused and stumble over my words because no matter how painfully I tried I wouldn't find any tangible evidence that I am her, that nameless girl. Why did he leave her with no name? Is it because he wanted to write about me? But he wouldn't dare to call her Sulayma, of course, and if he chose another name for her, his imagination would be obstructed and fall into disarray. That's probably why he left her with no definite name. But she's me! It's true that she belongs to another family, and lived a completely different memory. But our souls glide through the same constellations. I haven't told him. I don't have a strong enough argument. Perhaps he'll tell me that we belong to the same generation and live in the same city, and share some general details common to all Syrians, as well as both visiting Kameel. I wouldn't know how to explain to him that our resemblance doesn't stem from these things, not even our visits to Kameel. There's something deeper than generation, country, and doctor. I noticed the language of his novel. I found nothing but diary entries written in a journalistic language that has no freshness. As if, in his inability to write a novel about the revolution, he chose to write a diary to justify his own inadequacy to himself.

to exist. Sulayma, who loves him, is likewise alienated, a physician in the grip of fear just like her father, who is scared and anguished, like she imagines men to be, tormented like those she meets in the clinic of Kameel the psychiatrist.

Sulayma decides to complete Naseem's unfinished novel from her own perspective. She is almost certain he wrote it about her, rather than about some other young woman living a different life in a family unrelated to her own. Fear itself is concentrated in the strange young woman that Naseem made his novel's protagonist. She is Sulayma's double in her fear, her anxiety, and her alienation. Sulayma tries to find her, to prove that someone such as this, bodily and spiritually other than her, yet who resembles her to this extent, really exists distinct from her, someone whom she may not know at all.

Dima Wannous

RASHA OMRAN

The woman who lived in the house before me

A POEM,

TRANSLATED BY JONATHAN WRIGHT

Whenever I start writing anything about love, the wild woman's fingers reach
    out and push my fingers off the keyboard . . . the wild woman
the wild one
who looks like me

* * *

There's a big mirror by the bedroom door
Whenever I stand in front of it
I see the face of the woman who lived in the house before me
the woman I don't know
but I'm discovering her secrets in detail
story by story
whenever I stand in front of the mirror
the big mirror by the bedroom door
the one put up by the solitary woman who lived in the house before me

* * *

If it was me who'd lived in the house before her
I would have done the same thing:
taken the "magic eye" peephole out of the front door
and left the hole uncovered
so that an ordinary eye could come

and peep in
on my solitude

* * *

As I opened the front door, coming back from a long night out, I saw her
waiting for me behind the door, a gloating smile on her face as if she were
saying: "Everything you're doing is nonsense. I know all about it, going out
with friends, a late night drink, flirting with drunks in a cramped bar, the
text messages you send every hour. Only here, where you live, there's
plenty of space for you to examine your body and writhe to yourself like a
snake in the basket of some snake-charmer, a man without features who
plays on the flute." She said this, then disappeared, leaving traces of her
gloating smile scattered from the front door to the bed in the dark
bedroom. All I did was pick my way between her gloating smiles, then go
to sleep in bed, hugging my pillow in case some death caught me on my
own at first light.

* * *

In the middle of the dining room, on the white tiles, there's a large rust-
coloured stain. Every day I try in vain to get it off the tiles. Only today I
thought of using a sharp knife to remove it. While I was scraping it with the
knife blade I saw the trace of lines that look like an eye with a big black
pupil oozing rust. Maybe it's the eye of the woman who lived in the house
before me and maybe she, like me, pulled out one of her eyes and threw it
into the middle of the room. She was trying to reach halfway to oblivion –
the oblivion that a woman usually starts with her eyes once she has put her
heart on the table, surrounded with bread and salt and lemons for a dinner
that will be the last before she settles down alone in the ashtray.

* * *

My head is lying on the bed
my feet are pulled upwards
and my arms are touching the ceiling
Only my body is suspended in the void
in a scene like a rocking cradle.
Right on top of me is a long red dress,
as if abandoned in this magnificent empty space
for one female body to fly towards it
while the head lying on the pillow gradually changes
as the reflection of the faint candle-light changes in the darkness on the
    ceiling

* * *

Women poets are like solitary cats. When they find open doors, they slip
through without anyone seeing, but they soon come back disappointed and
make do with their own claw mark on their flesh – the mark that will stay
forever, like a polished mirror that shows up the flaws in the faces that stand
in front of it a while. Then they run out through open doors without leaving
a trace behind them.

* * *

I said to the man who was with me:
We women reproduce spontaneously
as if we were a single womb
as if my grandmother were my daughter
We are as streamlined as a field snake
and as cold as marble under a pot that has just come out of the oven
The only difference
is the ability to sew up the longest split seam under the left breast.

* * *

Around my neck I put the silver crocodile I bought from the man who sells
old bric-a-bric. But as I was opening the front door to go out the chain
around my neck broke and the silver crocodile fell to the floor. The sharp
sound as it hit the tiles was enough to make my heart fall to the ground with
the crocodile by the door. What I did was I picked up the heart, hung it on
the wall in an old wooden frame that already held the heart of a woman
who looks like me, and went out. There was a white butterfly with delicate
wings approaching the empty space on my left side and trying to come in

* * *

I put on her nightshirt, which had been left in the wall closet, and went to
sleep. In the night I woke up to the sound of a man breathing. His face
wrapped in rough woollen yarn, he was sleeping beside me. When I took
off the shirt, completing the nightly ritual, the man suddenly slipped out of
bed and left, and I went back to sleep. The next morning I found the
nightshirt folded in the closet, and on the bed there was a ball of rough
woollen yarn. The woman who lived in the house before me used to unravel
the yarns with her fingers with astonishing proficiency and then reknit
them in the form of a tiny man with big feet and a face with blank features

* * *

So I open my front door wide and count the grains of sand that have come in,
one by one, and when I tire of counting I stretch out right across the
threshold and pile the sand up on top of my body, while the woman who
lived in the house before me picks up her old broom and removes the sand
from the floor, as is proper for a solitary homemaker who is well aware that

the thresholds made by women to relax on are just grains of piled-up sand that will blow away as soon as the door opens a little, leaving love and loneliness to collide as they pass through the doorway.

* * *

It means nothing for us to be solitary women
We are like bamboo stalks and, if we wanted, we could make do with water,
    for our tips to turn green
and in our prejudices we take hold of volcanoes
and put our hearts at the bottom of their earth
close to the point of friction that produces the great fire
and when everything comes to an end
we rise like immortal trees in the midst of ruin
witness to the sources of sadness and death
It means nothing for us to be solitary
We can play with dough for the rest of our lives wherever we are
I was saying this on the phone to my friend this morning as she packed her
    bags towards a different solitude
while the woman who lived in the house before me
stood right behind me
with her hands in my hair
pulling the white threads of disappointment that are wrapped round my head
every night
when I go to sleep like a solitary woman
hugging her cold pillow

* * *

All I did tonight was spread my life on the table like a newspaper full of crossword puzzles. Then I started to think about the missing words, and so I spent the time writing letters in the empty squares and then rubbing them out. I did this all evening while the woman who lived in the house before me picked the little crumbs of rubber off the table and put them in an old white handkerchief with a hole in the middle like another empty square in the crossword puzzle.

* * *

We make sure we put fresh flowers in the vase every day
and we make sure we change the colours of the cushions on the sofa
and put scented candles at the thresholds of the rooms
and rearrange the bed covers in the morning
We make sure we do everything that makes us forget we are solitary women
But when passing men follow the scent of violets that blows through our
   windows
we shut the windows tight
and embrace the disappointments we've accumulated
Then we pour water on the fading violets
and so
the scene repeats itself day after day
like an old film where nobody notices that dust has ruined the final scenes

* * *

Women poets are mad. They are well aware that they are not trees, yet every
night they take off their tattered clothes and hang amulets on their breasts,
then stand up naked in the moonlight. So when they see their long shadows
immobile in the darkness they think they are trees and they start rustling.
Women poets are mad. They don't know that the rustling of the trees does
not attract trusting birds and that their shadows will disappear as soon as a
passing cloud blocks out the moonlight. Women poets are mad. In the
morning they won't remember what they did the night before, yet when
they stand in front of their mirrors, they will notice deep scars on their
breasts, exactly where their lost amulets were hanging.

* * *

Women poets are dreamers. They come back home at the end of the night
expecting to find stars waiting for them on the doorstep and coloured
butterflies that will light up their beds. But when they open their front
doors, they grope the walls as if blind until they reach their bedrooms.
Women poets are dreamers. They'll go to sleep in the belief that their
familiar smells will ward off nightmares and that in the morning they will
find their hearts still in place, not thrown on the ground like old clothes.
Women poets are dreamers. They think the holes in their breasts are
cigarette burns they hadn't noticed when they were lost in a wine-induced
stupor. But they will wake up in the morning and discover the gaps in their

left sides, gaps as deep as vast deserts where the sand blows in from all directions.

* * *

Women poets break their promises whenever they say they'll turn tame, the timid women poets who do not try to hide the howling of their hungry veins. So they remain solitary, like wolves that can no longer find what satisfies their fangs' desire to bite.

* * *

There's nothing under my fingers
I spread the palm of my hand flat on the tiles, then lift it up to see what trace
  it has left
There's no trace of my hand on the tiles
nor on the walls where I have long left fingerprints in various colours
It seems to me
that my fingers are like water
and the marks they leave are soon erased by the heat of the place
the same place I sit when I'm shivering from cold
as if I were a bird of passage
coming through an open window
then caught in a little room
tracing on its walls coloured maps
that disappear and reappear
and disappear again
without leaving any trace of a shadow to shelter the bird of passage.

* * *

Don't say anything
This world is full of noise
Listen to it and don't say anything
If you like, just whisper your stories in the ear of the dust
in the ear of a suicidal butterfly
One day
when everyone falls silent
your whisperings will grow like sugarcane stalks

and the butterflies will circle around them
and back to the void will go your stories about the solitary women
who cut off their fingers
and hung them on washing lines
for the sun to dry off the traces of damp
on the empty beds

* * *

Love is nothing but a plague
says Anne Sexton
as she says goodbye to the world before her suicide
while I, who cannot endure death,
want to put love in the vase
and change the water every five days
and watch its shadow stretched across the wall in the darkness
I want to hang it on the washing line
for the birds to stand on it without fear
I want to grow it as a tree in the bedroom
a tall tree
and whenever I feel in despair
I'd tie a silk handkerchief around my neck
and hang it from the highest branch in the tree
and leave it there
That way I'll keep my head alive
while my body, dead by suicide,
lies on an empty bed
in a bedroom
that solitary women usually pass on, one to another

* * *

Solitary women resume their lives
They bring flowers to their houses
and decorate their kitchens with fruit that will wilt in a while
and change their perfumes so that no one smell clings to their lovers' shirts
They listen to Umm Kalthoum with the passion of teenagers
and read about the lives of women poets who killed themselves, then smile
    that they are still alive

But when the darkness spreads
they invent a new kind of life
as if they're taking flowers to the bedrooms
and pouring bottles of perfume on the beds
and planting fruit on the pillows
In the morning they will have the impression
that gardens have sprung up in their rooms
and that some sunlight is getting through the dark curtains
and that death is just a toy, played with by those who enter the gardens
and that its dazzling teeth
are only a marvellous carving
that they bought one day
and left close to the gates
of their imaginary gardens

* * *

She was sitting by the door to the building
in an elegant black dress
with short silver hair
and signs of the many years on her thin cheeks
I don't know where he is, she said,
we argued like ordinary couples, as we've been arguing for the past forty
 years,
but he left home four hours ago and hasn't come back
After five hours of waiting
she went upstairs to her house
opened the door and went in
She looked at his picture hanging on the wall
She fetched a clean handkerchief
and wiped the dust off it
Then she rearranged the pale black sash draped over the corner of the picture
and, with astonishing normality, went to sleep
like any solitary woman
She no longer distinguishes
between hours and years
The only difference is
that she's going to wake up in the morning
and say: "Good morning"

as she looks at a picture of a solitary man
hanging on the wall

* * *

I was going to say:
Bury me there, where I always wanted to be, under the shade of some tree.
   Maybe I'll go back into the chlorophyll of the leaves, or into the water
   seeping into the trunk. I don't like nothingness, yet the ground there has
   been dried by death and no longer produces anything but nothingness. I
   don't like nothingness.
I was going to say:
Bury me here, where my heart desires, maybe I'll change back into a drop of
   water in the great river, but the dead don't change back, and the ground is
   layers of sand. I don't like sand.
I was going to say:
Tie a rock to me and throw my body into the sea, into the deep sea. It's
   nobler to be eaten by a savage shark than to be eaten by worms, but the sea
   was overflowing with humans and there was a big banquet on. I don't like
   to intrude on big banquets.
I was going to say:
Turn my body into a bomb and have me blow up whoever you want. Then
   there'll only be very very little of me left but I'm worried that little of me
   will stick in the memory of some murderer. I don't like murderers.
I was going to say:
Burn my body and scatter the ashes from the top of that mountain in
   Damascus. Maybe some of the dust will land on the shoulder of the person
   I love there,
but I know this is a heavy burden on your convictions. I don't like heavy
   people.
I will say:
If I die, put my body in some remote desert where wolves will come and tear
   into it, and I won't object and I won't feel anything but contented, and
   maybe I'll feel amused in that empty space, since there'd be someone to
   relieve the loneliness of my death by biting
Women poets usually don't like the loneliness of death.

* * *

I don't own many things
some white roses I put in a vase and watch how their leaves fall off day by day
a white cat that waits for me behind the door when I stagger home
a bedcover stained with the smell of the last man I loved
a white heart in which repeated disappointments have dug their fingernails
black kohl that I leave on my eyes when I go to sleep
and, like all solitary women,
I dream of the white angel that visits me in the middle of the night:
he wipes the kohl from my eyes
he puts my heart back in its natural state
he wraps me in a white gown that's immaculate
and puts his fresh roses in my hands
then he hands me over to nothingness
and disappears.
And when I wake up the next morning
I look in the mirror
and see dry lips that no one has kissed, not even a goodbye kiss
and I see faraway eyes
like the eyes of a cat that has rolled its face in the ashes
and on the bed
there's a heart wrapped in wilting rose leaves
while the room fills with the smell of the last man I loved
as if it's the only sign of the void
the void to which I will surrender
in the night to come

* * *

Women poets are crafty. They knew that their solitude is like a rabid dog that
nothing can stop barking. So whenever they fall in love with a man they put
their solitude out of its misery with a bullet. Women poets are crafty. They
knew they're like water, that will slip through the fingers whenever a
strong fist tries to hold it, and so they're used to covering their solitude in
a bullet-proof jacket. Women poets are crafty. They're well aware that if
they killed their solitude they would just be widows who dress in mourning
and weave shrouds with rough wool while waiting for someone to die.

KHALED KHALIFA

Death
is Hard Work

A CHAPTER FROM THE NOVEL,
TRANSLATED BY LERI PRICE

Photo by Samuel Shimon

Chapter One
If you were a sack of cumin

Two hours before he died, Abdel Latif Al Salim looked his son Belbol straight in the eye with as much of his remaining strength as he could muster, as if extracting a solemn vow, and he repeated his request to be buried in the cemetery of Anabiya. After all this time, his bones would rest in his home village beside the ashes of his sister Layla, he said; he almost added, beside her scent, but he hadn't been sure that the dead would smell the same after forty years. He considered these few words a final command and added nothing which might lend them an ambiguous interpretation. He had resolved to be silent in his last hours. He closed his eyes, ignoring the people around him, and sank into his solitude with a smile. He recalled an image of Nevine, her smile, her scent, her naked body wrapped in a black abaya as she tried to float like a butterfly. He remembered how his eyes had gleamed at that moment, how his heart thudded, and his knees trembled, and how he carried her to the bed and kissed her greedily, and before he could recall every moment of that 'night of immortal secrets', as they used to call it, he died.

Belbol, in a rare moment of courage and under the influence of his father's parting words and sad, misted eyes, acted firmly and without fear. He promised his father he would carry out his instruction, which, despite being clear and simple, would be a hard task. It was natural that a man, with much reason to lament and knowing he would die within hours, should be weak and make requests which would be difficult to carry out; equally, it was natural for a man to put on a cheerful front, as Belbol was doing, so as not to forsake him. The last moment was always the most sentimental, usually an inappropriate time for reflection; it held no room for rational judgement, because time had solidified within it. Peace and deliberation were required for reviewing the past and settling accounts, neither of which were practised by those approaching death. They hastily threw off their burdens and crossed the isthmus, to the other side where time had no value.

Belbol, later, regretted having not been more resolute. He should have told his father how difficult it would be to carry out his instruction in days like these. Battle casualties everywhere were buried in mass graves without having their identities picked out. Mourning ceremonies, even those of rich families, were curtailed to a few hours. Death was no longer a carnival worthy of proclaiming prestige; a few roses, a few mourners yawning in a half-empty living room for a couple of hours, someone reciting a sura or two from the Qur'an in a low voice, and that was it.

Belbol thought that a silent funeral removed the awe of the dead person. For the first time, everyone was equal in death. Rites and rituals meant nothing now: the poor and the rich, the officers and infantry in the regime's army, armed squadron commanders, fighters, the passers-by and the unidentified, all were buried in pitiful processions. Death was no longer an act which commanded distress; it had become an escape which roused envy in the living.

As for Belbol, the story was very different. His father's body was a heavy burden. In a fleeting, sentimental moment Belbol had promised to bury him in the same tomb as his Aunt Layla, whom he didn't even know. He had thought that his father would ask for a safeguard of the rights of his new wife, Nevine, in the family home. The building had been totally destroyed in an air raid, apart from the bedroom where his father had passed his last days of love with Nevine before leaving the village of S with the help of opposition fighters.

Belbol would never forget that scene. His father had been clean and neat when the fighters brought him, and it was clear they had looked after their comrade well, when he had chosen to stay with them despite the siege which had been imposed on S for more than three years. They bid him an affectionate goodbye, kissed him warmly, and saluted him. After enjoining Belbol to care for him properly, they vanished in the blink of an eye through a well-guarded side road which revealed the orchards leading back to the village. His father's eyes were gleaming for the last time as he tried to raise his hand to wave to them, but couldn't. He was exhausted and starving, having lost more than half his bodyweight; like everyone under siege, it had been months since he had eaten a full meal.

His body was laid out on a metal stretcher in the public hospital. The doctor said to Belbol: "Many people die every day. Be happy he reached old age." Belbol was not quite as happy as the doctor wished, but he understood what had been meant. He felt suffocated by this dilemma; the city streets were deserted after eight in the evening, and he had to move the body before midday tomorrow. The body couldn't take up space in the morgue for long; a large consignment of soldiers' bodies would arrive at dawn from the outskirts of Damascus, where the battles never stopped.

When Belbol left the hospital it was almost two o'clock in the morning. He thought that his father had made a demand of the whole family, and that every member had a responsibility to carry out his last wish. He looked for a taxi to go to his brother Hussein's house after successive attempts to call him had failed. He considered sending Hussein an SMS but conveying the news of a father's death by text message was contemptible. He had to say it face to face, and accept his share of the pain.

The soldiers guarding the hospital waved at him to turn towards neighbouring Daraa Station – he would find a taxi there. Belbol decided not to dwell on the sound of bullets near at hand. He put his hands in his pockets, quickened his pace, and abandoned his fear. Such a walk on this winter night was extremely hazardous; the patrols never stopped, and the streets were crammed with anonymous armed men. Electricity had been cut off in most areas, concrete blocks were piled high in front of the security checkpoints that occupied most roads. No one, if they weren't a resident, could have known the passages where it was permitted to walk and the passages where it was forbidden. From a distance Belbol saw a few men gathered in a circle around an upturned petrol drum in which some firewood had been set alight. He guessed that they were mostly taxi drivers who had paused at the end of their journeys and were waiting for dawn to go home. The last glimmer of his bravery had almost flickered out by the time he found one, serenely listening to Um Kulthum. Belbol quickly reached an understanding with him and didn't dispute the fare that was asked.

They were silent at first, and after a few minutes Belbol wanted to rid himself of his fear. He told the driver that his father had died an hour ago in the hospital, of old age. The driver laughed and informed him that three of his brothers and their children had died a month before in an airstrike. Both were silent; the conversation was no longer on an even footing. Belbol waited a while before sympathising with him, as he was decent with him, and didn't drive away until he had seen Belbol was safe inside. Hussein opened the door and when he saw Belbol standing there at that time of the morning, he knew what had happened. He hugged his brother affectionately, led him inside and made him some tea. He asked if Belbol wanted to wash his face, and promised to take care of everything that still needed to be done: finding a shroud, making the burial arrangements, and fetching their sister Fatima.

Belbol felt himself lighter and braver, the burden of his cares lifted. He forgot that Hussein had ignored his father when he was in hospital; the important thing was he hadn't followed this up by disappearing and abandoning him. Belbol was confident in his brother's ability to manage situations such as these. Hussein had roamed between several trades which had gained him experience in the dealings of the state, and he had contacts all over the place. Without delay, Hussein dismantled two seats from his microbus and re-arranged them in the shape of an open box. He said: "We will lie the body on the side seat, and there will be enough space for everyone to travel comfortably." He meant Belbol and their sister Fatima; if their in-laws wanted to accompany them, they wouldn't be in the way. This idea was soon rejected: people no longer felt it necessary to undertake a duty towards a man whose corpse had hundreds of kilometres to travel before his final resting place.

By seven o'clock, Hussein had finished all the arrangements for the journey. He had brought his sister from her house and erased the signs on his microbus, which he used to work the Jaramana line. With the help of a car electrician friend, he had improvised an ambulance siren from the microbus horn. He also bought an air freshener, which he supposed would be needed on the long journey, and didn't forget to call another of his friends to ensure four large blocks of ice were to hand. Despite the difficulty of what was demanded, his friends had woken before dawn, offered him their condolences and helped him arrange everything for the journey. The only thing still left to obtain, before they could be on their way, was the signature of the director of the hospital, who would not be in before 9 o'clock. They parked in front of the hospital gate to wait for him, but the morgue official asked them to move their father's body immediately, as a new consignment of bodies was waiting on the cold floor and the fridges were chock-full.

Belbol didn't dare accompany Hussein when he went into the morgue. The corridors were filled with the dark, sad faces of men and women waiting to receive the bodies of their loved ones. The orderly gestured that he should search the southern side of the morgue, and Hussein almost threw up as he opened the crammed in boxes. Finally, after he had almost lost hope he found his father's fresh corpse; hundreds of bodies had been lost and forgotten in this chaos. It was clear that his father had not been dead for long. Hussein slipped 3,000 lira to the official so that the orderly would be allowed to help him wash and shroud the body in the filthy bathroom reserved for the dead, who no longer cared whether it was clean or not. The scene in the morgue was horrifying. Officers were walking through the corridors and speaking angrily, cursing the armed opposition fighters. Troops in full combat gear were wandering around aimlessly, smelling of battle. They had brought their friends, either wounded or killed, and dawdling was their chance to escape or postpone returning to where death lay in wait for them. Everything in this turmoil seemed very near to death.

Hussein arranged his father's body in the front seat in such a way that he wouldn't see him and be distracted whenever he looked in the mirror. He asked Fatima to be quiet, even though she hadn't said a word, but her sobbing grew louder. Since their childhood Hussein had enjoyed ordering her about, and Fatima obeyed him without dispute; compliance with her brother's demands gave her a sense of equilibrium and protection. Hussein was furious at Belbol whom he saw leaning against a distant wall and smoking as if he didn't have a care in the world. He slammed the door of the bus and went back to the hospital gate to wait for the director, who had to sign the death certificate before the official proceedings were over. It wasn't exactly the place to make small talk, but he couldn't help asking a woman, who was also waiting, if she knew when the director was expected. She shrugged to show that she didn't know and turned her face away. Hussein didn't attempt to speak again to anyone else although he hated waiting in silence, believing that speaking would have alleviated their misery. He could feel the tension and anger hidden in the eyes of the petitioners who were crammed into the corridor. At nine o'clock, the director arrived and signed the death certificate. Immediately, Hussein asked Belbol to get in the bus; at the same time, he asked Fatima firmly to cover the body with the blankets he had brought from his house, and to shut up.

Hussein informed his siblings that removing the body had cost them ten thousand lira, adding that every detail had been recorded in a small accounts book. Without waiting for comments, he fell to thinking of the quickest way out of Damascus. At this time of the morning, the roads were full of traffic and the many checkpoints were jammed; it might take hours. He continued his calculations, based on his experience as a microbus driver who worked in traffic all day. The road through Abbasiyin Square would be best, although the security checks had a bad reputation in this area. He told himself that just thinking of how to cross Sabaa Bahrat Square in the city centre would be a disaster.

Hussein decided to leave Damascus through Abbasiyin Square and tried to follow close behind an ambulance. The first checkpoint wouldn't allow him the whole way along the road, but he did achieve some distance. The ambulance siren was no use whatsoever – no one made way for him. Amid the crowds and the chaos, Hussein reflected that a funeral procession would have generated more sympathy in peacetime – cars used to pull over, passers-by used to stop and cast genuinely sympathetic looks – but in war, a funeral procession was a regular occurrence that aroused only envy in the living, whose lives were now spent in miserable anticipation of death.

A queue of ambulances suddenly descended on him, heading out of the city. They contained soldiers who were accompanying coffins; he could see them through a small window. Hussein tried to sneak in between the vehicles but an angry yell and a cocked weapon from one of the furious soldiers returned him to the line of normal traffic. When the last ambulance in the queue arrived next to him, it slowed down and a soldier leaned out of the window, spat copiously on him, and added a string of curses. Hussein looked at the spittle that moistened his arm and was flooded with rage; at that moment he wanted to cry. Belbol kept quiet and averted his face so as not to increase his brother's embarrassment at being insulted. Fatima no longer felt like crying; she was surprised at how few tears she had shed. She put off expressing her sadness and loss until the burial, the most keenly felt part of saying goodbye.

Since childhood, Hussein had been in the habit of memorising entire pages of cheap almanacs published by Islamic philanthropic organisations, which contained famous sayings, aphorisms, verses from the Qur'an, and hadiths of the Prophet. He would use them in his everyday speech to give his audience the impression of being widely read. He always used to believe that he had not been created to live on the margins as a mere observer, but at that moment, looking at the deluge of vehicles inundating Abbasiyin Square, he felt terrifyingly powerless; he couldn't find an appropriate aphorism to break the strident silence overpowering his brother and sister, and he wanted them to forget he had been spat upon. He tried to remember sayings about death and couldn't come up with anything apart from "The living outlast the dead". He didn't like this one because of how often it was used by cowards – today might be a different matter, and it would be the dead that "outlasted" the living. He went on to muse that they would all die in the not-too-distant future. This thought had given him exceptional courage over the previous four years, and not only had it increased his stoicism daily, but he was more able to withstand the insults he received in the course of his work from soldiers and mukhabarat at the checkpoints. He took the view that they would die today or tomorrow, or next month at the latest, and they would not go back home to their families. It was a heavy nightmare but true, and all felt its weight. Every inhabitant of the city regarded each other as pre-dead, and so found relief from their irritation and anger.

The bus crawled painfully slowly towards the hundreds of vehicles flooding Abbasiyin Square. From a distance, three Suzuki pickup trucks with hoisted flags gleamed; elderly men were standing in their open backs and trying to clear the road. One of them yelled through a loudhailer, loud and clear: "Martyrs, martyrs, martyrs." He followed this up furiously with: "Make way for the martyrs, make way for the martyrs." But no one cared. The Suzuki trucks inched closer to Hussein's microbus as they tried to escape the snarl of traffic.

Hussein said that they were coming from Tishreen Military Hospital, and added that the poor couldn't even find an ambulance to take them to their grave. Belbol's eyes remained glued to the man who carried the loudhailer until he was lost from view.

Belbol reflected that he was totally unable to escape from death. It was a terrifying deluge surrounding everyone. He recalled when the regime used to go overboard in the commemorative funerals it held for its fallen. On television, the official band of these ceremonies would play the "Martyr's Song", and place on every coffin a large bouquet bearing the name of the Commander-in-Chief of the Army and the Armed Forces (who was also the President), and another bouquet in the name of the Minister of Defence, and a third in the name of their comrades-in-arms in their squadron or department. The female broadcaster would loudly announce the name, function and rank of the martyr, and the television would broadcast a shot of the family as they declared how proud they were, how glorious it was that their son had been martyred in the course of faithfully laying down his life for the nation and the Leader. Always those two words – nation and Leader – were inseparable on television. After several months, the band, the bouquets and the flag disappeared; so did the female broadcasters vaunting impoverished boys martyred for their loyalty to the nation and the Leader; so did all reverence for the word "martyr". Belbol looked at the city, which was vanishing from sight now. He remembered how passionately his colleagues used to recount stories of how bodies weren't being looked for or buried properly. They would talk angrily about the hospitals stuffed with the dead. Searching for a body had become hard work, even more so when the families, immediately upon being informed of the death of their sons, were forced to go to the barracks and look for their bodies, which had earlier been buried in mass graves, or lost among devastated buildings and the iron skeletons of tanks and burned-out guns. Even these stories eventually lost their shine, and no one told them any more. Worst of all, in this war, was the way that the exceptional became habitual and tragedies were mundane. Thus, as Belbol looked at his father, he felt his distinction; at least this body was surrounded by the care of its three children, and not left to the elements. He almost told Hussein and Fatima about their father's last moments – he was surprised he hadn't already done so – but held back, convinced that they had a long way to go, and there would be time enough to talk about the exploits of the departed, and to recall a past that had never been unhappy.

Hussein was annoyed at himself. The thousands of sayings and aphorisms he had learned by heart over twenty years had been of no use in expressing his predicament in this traffic, but he refused to surrender to his bad memory. He repeated a few sayings on different topics such as unfaithfulness, and hope, and the betrayal of friends. He considered this a useful exercise for his memory; he might need these sayings in a few hours, and they needed to be primed and on hand. He remembered a few lines of Ahmed Shawqi and repeated them forcefully, with stately pronunciation: "Crimson freedom has a door / knocked by every blood-stained hand . . ." With some difficulty he remembered the following line: ". . . he will ever dwell among the pits." But he had mixed up Shawqi with a line from Shabi's poem "If one day the people wish to live." This combination pleased him; it didn't strike him as a mistake that he wanted to combine two poems with different rhyme schemes. He had in fact read these lines dozens of times in the pages of the almanacs, and had liked them very much; he used them to insult cowards. He repeated both imperfect lines in a murmur as if in lament for his revolutionary father. Belbol didn't care; he was content with the three previous months he and his father had spent talking over everything. Fatima understood the recitation as a belated reconciliation between Hussein and his father. She wanted to bless it, but Belbol's heavy silence made her hesitate and she decided to wait for a more suitable opportunity to voice her opinion on the long rift between Hussein and his father. True, it had passed through different stages and they had occasionally approached each other and tried to turn over a new leaf, but their relationship never went back to its cloudless beginnings, when Hussein had been the spoiled favourite.

The soldiers at the last checkpoint before leaving Damascus made do with a cursory glance over the papers and allowed them to pass. Many corpses were leaving the city today, and just as many were coming in. The sight of them was abhorrent for the mud-spattered soldiers; the bodies heralded their own oncoming death, which they also wanted not to think about. Hussein didn't look at his watch. He heaved a sigh of relief; he was already delivered from the traffic of Abbasiyin Square, and Damascus was falling behind them. They had to arrive at Anabiya before midday. Fatima and Belbol regained their optimism and reviewed the necessities for their journey: bottles of mineral water, cigarettes, identity cards and the little money they had left.

He would be buried at the right time, Belbol told himself. The body wouldn't rot in this cold winter. They were fortunate he hadn't died in August, when flies tore at the dead. Death was solitary at all times, but on occasion it was a heavy burden on the living. There was a difference between an old man who died in his village, surrounded by family and close to the cemetery, and another who died hundreds of kilometres away from them all. The hardship of the living differed from that of the dead; no one wants a loved one to be destined to rot. They want him to look his best in death for that final image which cannot be erased from memory. It is the declaration of humanity's salvation which the sorrowing being's image preserves when his muscles slacken in sadness; and the image of the depressed being, whose melancholy never lifts from his features, is generally like an image of birth.

At the checkpoint outside the gate to Damascus, just before the turning onto the highway, the soldier nodded inside the bus and enquired what was beneath the blanket. Belbol said calmly: "It's my father's body." The soldier asked the question again more emphatically, pointing to the heavy pile of blankets, and Belbol re-affirmed his answer. The soldier motioned to Hussein to proceed into the Goods to Declare lane, where public transport vehicles were lined up and a soldier, who was about twenty years old, was circling each one with a bomb detector. The soldier left the checkpoint and went inside a one-room building, previously a workshop and now used as an office and barracks for the checkpoint soldiers. After a few minutes, an officer marched towards the microbus, wrenched open the door and ordered them to uncover the body. Belbol lifted the blanket from his father's face. It was still fresh, his death still raw and tender. With studied callousness, the officer demanded the official documentation for the body, and Fatima presented him with the death certificate signed by the Director of the Public Hospital and the morgue official, together with their identity cards. He scrutinised the identity cards, and surprised them by asking for the identity card of the dead man as well. Belbol almost explained that all corpses possess one name, that they slip away from their history and their past to affirm their belonging to one family, the family of the dead, and that no dead person has any other identity paper than a death certificate. But Fatima slipped the identity card from her bag and offered it to the officer, who peered at the face of the body and the picture on his identity card which had been taken twenty years before. At that time he had often laughed; now, his face bore the signs of a stern, tough man. The officer took the identity cards and went back to his room. The three of them exchanged glances, and decided to wait in the bus without moving.

Translated from the author's novel *Al-Mawt A'malun Shaq* (Death is Hard Work), published by Hachette Antoine, Beirut 2015

HALA MOHAMMAD

Lend me the window, stranger

FROM THE POEM,
TRANSLATED BY RAPHAEL COHEN

HALA MOHAMMAD

1

The house changed so much
after leaving.
I changed.
Syria changed:
the neighbours' houses, the streets,
the quarters.
All the places in the world become a passing moment
whereas love
gains its strength from us always fearing it might leave
when we know how much we long for it to stay.

The house changed so much.
Syria changed:
the neighbours' houses, the quarters,
the streets
with their shade panting close to you like a puppy
– which your high heels
your Chanel dresses
and handbags all knew –
the earrings and bracelets in
the goldsmiths' market and your golden laughter.

The house changed so much after your leaving.
Syria changed,
and the neighbours' houses and the streets.
. . .
How can I tell you
how make your death anxious?
. . .
Syria has been demolished by war,
and memories, Mother dearest,
do not a country make.

2

The wedding couches

you re-upholstered three times before I left home,
couches from Chez Maurice
I saw in Paris
seating another mother like you
with your plaits tied in a bunch behind
and the delicious smell of your cooking.
Like you she wore a smile —
like yours in the doorway
that lit up the neighbours as they climbed seven floors without a lift.

Palm-sized,
the wooden doorknob
bears your imprint.

3

One day I will stretch out my hand
into this existence
and open the front door.
The dust will rise
and fall into my arms
and we will cry, I and desolation.
Calmly, I will go into the house
and see it as I have never seen it before.
The oh-so patient walls will sigh.
I will take my picture with every particle of life
documenting
as if there was a revolution.

4

The most beautiful marble I laid on the doorstep,
old yellowish marble.
I attached a new padlock at the foot of the door,
a yellowish copper padlock.
I locked up the house and its contents
that yellowish afternoon

and in the eye of the setting sun
I locked the door on the dust that gathered to say goodbye,
        yellowish dust,
and withdrew from my own life.
When from afar I see
the living room, the mirrors
the curtains
my dresses in the wardrobes
the kitchen plates
the tea kettle
the yellowish wooden dining table
the elegant wickerwork chairs
fracturing the sunlight,
scattering it over the tiles
as a carpet of light
underneath the table legs,
and the black television
silent
I do not want this poem to end
as I pen it.
I want to remain suspended in this space
the space that empties my mind of thought
turns my mind into a heart.

One heart attack
for all this love
is not enough.

5

Under the olive tree
the grave blooms
butterflies
bees
ants
. . .
and shade.

6

Seasons pass by before us, slowly pass by
on the howdah of time, pass by
overflowing with shadows, pass by
overflowing with promises and flowers, pass by
before our demolished houses
before the camps,
in prisons,
in agony . . . pass by
in dreams, pass by
hours, seconds, and instants like bullets, pass by
and this death   impatient
to reach the far bank of the story . . .
passes by.

7

The war is over, my love, and no one has gone home –
even the homes are not back from the war.
The way back didn't know the way.
The rabbits in the fields
under weeds incinerated by napalm, chlorine gas and sarin
shut their eyes in front of the cameras
not wanting to be photographed.
The world does not know our story
the children died

To whom then to tell stories?

LYRICS (1)

War is back for the thousandth time
and for the thousandth time
perhaps we will live.
For the thousandth time

we gamble what we have
we gamble the songs
hurling them at barrel-bombs and jets,
at the sniper on the roof of the house
at inter-continental missiles
We hurl them at the picture of the tyrant wearing his dark glasses
on an electricity pylon
and hurl them at this sanctuary of death
which draws nearer
draws nearer

the songs.

LYRICS (2)

All that I have left of you:
poems.
When they want they swell in my chest and stab.
They press under my fingers
and touch comes alive
they wait for me at the junction
between night and day
they come in the chaos of destruction
and dust
they come after every bombardment
carrying me on the back of a cloud
they wake me up from sleep
dusty with rhythm
with wild flowers
with rapture.

You send what you can smuggle out to us
and with your heavy anklets of fire
you climb the stairway to massacre alone,
O Syria.

15

My house had windows
that overlooked cypress and poplar trees.
The windows borrowed shade for the house from the trees
and the trees rustled with secrets.
When the soldiers attacked our house
they were shocked it was not destroyed
they were shocked it was not in ruins.

Our clothes
are worn by butterflies

The silence about the waist
is poetry.

16

The grandmother said:
For a hundred years
you have guarded my grave

The butterfly said: Granny.

24

Lend me the window, stranger
Lend it to me right now
I beg you
Listen to me at sunset,
sunset over Syria.

MAHA HASSAN

Aleppo Metro

AN EXCERPT FROM THE FIRST CHAPTER OF THE NOVEL,
TRANSLATED BY JONATHAN WRIGHT

Half past nine in the morning

Susan sends me a message on Viber: "Are you at home? Call me." I call my sister and listen to the daily litany of moaning and weeping. It's a déja vu I've been going through every day with Susan for about a year. Forty days after my father died, Susan went to Turkey. She left Syria with her husband, her husband's father and my brother Samir. The others continued on their way to Europe using forged passports for which they paid large sums of money to mafias skilled in forging documents and sending Syrians to Europe. Samir had sold his house in Aleppo and invested the money in five foreign passports, for himself, his wife Jamila, their twin daughters Farah and Marah, who were two years old, and their four-year-old son Walid.

Susan and her husband Lorca didn't have enough money to travel by air on forged passports. Lorca left with his father and Susan stayed in Istanbul, waiting for Lorca to obtain a residence permit so that she could join him later. This was common practice: tens of thousands of Syrian women were sitting in Turkish towns and cities waiting to be reunited with their husbands. The children waver between two lives: a temporary life in Turkey and the life they anticipate in Sweden, Germany, Belgium, Switzerland, Denmark or Holland.

Some of the children go to Syrian schools run by Syrian opposition groups and learn Turkish as well as the Syrian syllabus. They know, along with their parents, that this education won't help them much in Europe, because they will have to start a different education system there and learn a new foreign language.

The childen swing between Arabic and Turkish as they wait to be dragged away from both those languages to learn German, Swedish or Dutch.

Every day Susan tells me the same thing: "I'm in Istanbul and every day I wake up expecting news that I'll be leaving, either to Sweden or to go back to Syria. I'm halfway between Syria and not-Syria, between, on the one hand, Lorca getting a residence permit so that we can leave for Europe and set up a new life there, and then it would be difficult for us to go back to Syria, except as visitors, and, on the other hand, the war ending so that we can pack up and go back to Aleppo, even before Lorca.

"It's hard to live in a station not knowing which train you're going to take – bound for Europe or bound for Aleppo.

"Psychologically, my eyes are still on Aleppo. Europe, with its beauty, its security and its opennness, doesn't tempt me. If it wasn't for the children, maybe I'd stay in Istanbul station, waiting for the train to Aleppo.

"But Europe is the best destination for the children's sake, though I always hold out hope that it wouldn't be a final destination. The war in Syria has destroyed the children's schools, the classrooms and the whole education system:

About *Aleppo Metro*

On the first day of my arrival in Paris from Aleppo, thirteen years ago, a few hours after lodging my bags at home I ran out to ride the metro for the first time in my life. I was under a compelling feeling that I was in another world separate from the city of Paris, circumventing it but like umbilical cords, protecting and feeding it, and connecting its peripheries together.

The French metro always managed to detach me from its usual din and clamour, giving me ample room to concentrate on writing. It was as if those closely connected carriages offered me an exclusive space, in the midst of the din, where I could give free rein to my imagination and start to write.

Having left my homeland behind, I inevitably kept, throughout my years in France, drawing comparisons and contrasts, looking at aspects of life in Europe, and noting their absence in Syria. Among those was the metro. I often daydreamed of a metro running across Aleppo from the extreme east to the extreme west, acting like an umbilical cord feeding the city. For long years, Paris and Aleppo came mixed in my dreams.

it mustn't be allowed to ruin the future of those who have escaped and survived the war."

Susan usually has a magic touch and a blithe spirit. Sometimes she retrieves them in spite of her worries for her future and the future of her children. "Half the people in Syria are now Europeans. Imagine, that taxi driver, Abu Abdou, Fatima's husband, now has a German passport and he's saying, 'At our place in Germany'."

Susan cries and says, "I'm fed up. I don't have any money. I want to go back to Aleppo. Mother's all alone there and what am I going to do here? I'll go to Aleppo and I'll only leave when Lorca gets his residence."

"If I had any money," I say, "I'd come and stay, but I can't afford the airfare."

"If you have any money, instead of spending it on the airfare, you could send it to me. We've been eating potatoes, burghul and rice all month. Hafal and Naya don't say anything and I think they'll always depressed. Naya said she wanted us to go back to Aleppo. Grandma's alone there and that's not right."

Hafal comes to the phone and tells me enthusiastically about discovering the Istanbul metro system. He was talking with the same excitement as when he

When the war broke out and its fires reached Aleppo, I felt my novel was writing itself. That narrative — which I started writing on the first day of my arrival in Paris, when I took the metro for the first time — found a fertile soil in the war.

Nightmares, fears, panic, guilt feelings, hopes of reclaiming the country and bridging the yawning gap between it and the West, the state of homelessness the Syrians suddenly found themselves in, the world unable to bring fighting in my country to a halt, my fellow Syrians divided between staying in the hell-fire at home and fleeing to the West. All those details, which have obsessed me during the war in Syria, provided the setting for my novel. Thus, *Aleppo Metro* came into being.

It is a narrative of forced migration, of bewilderment and confusion, of apprehension of the new place and yearning for the deserted one. It is a purely Syrian narrative, depicting how vulnerable creatures are facing a savage war.

Maha Hassan

talks about football matches in which his favourite team, Real Madrid, is play-ing. "Auntie," he says, "the metro is amazing. Aren't you an engineer? Why don't you design a metro for Aleppo? When I grow up I want to study engi-neering, and I want to design a metro for Aleppo like the one in Istanbul."

Hafal has put his finger on my pain and my obsession: a metro in Aleppo!

Susan comes back on line to tell how warm the metro is and how it's a prac-tical and modern form of transport and at the same time a place for meetings. She describes it as a moving marketplace or a whole street that carries you along. "Imagine, in the metro you meet people who live in the same city as you without you knowing. Today I met a family that was talking Arabic. When I heard Arabic, I looked around to find out who was speaking and I found a woman who lives in the same building as us in Aleppo, Umm Ma'moun and her sons, Ma'moun and Raouf. Imagine!

"In the Turkish metro you can hear pleasant and familiar languages: Arabic and Kurdish, which my children understand better than me, and Turkish of course."

Then the tone of sadness returns to Susan's voice: "Why isn't Aleppo like this? Why have other people taken an interest in their countries and developed them, while we've ruined our country?"

I don't argue with Susan often because she contradicts herself twenty times an hour. She can hold several contradictory opinions. One moment she's in favour of the revolution because the regime is corrupt and tyrannical and re-presses all freedoms, and then she's against the revolution because it's brought destruction. One moment she's in favour of going back to Syria, because there's no substitute for one's own country, then she talks about the country being in ruins and the need to protect the children and ensure their future. Then she consoles herself, saying, "When they grow up, they'll go back to Syria and become engineers, doctors, musicians and creative people and make Syria nicer than any other country in the world." I leave her to console herself in her confusion. Samir contacts me on Facebook. I don't answer him but go on chatting with Susan.

When Susan arrived in Istanbul, she got in touch with Ibrahim, the son of a friend of one of my uncles. He works in a translation agency and his father is Turkish with Turkish nationality. My sister worked for him doing some com-puter and office work, leaving her seven-year-old twins, Hafal and Naya, with Malak, Ibrahim's wife. Malak's children went to school while my sister's chil-dren stayed at home.

My sister couldn't find work in her own field. Opening a clinic in Turkey requires money and all the money had evaporated because of the war. To work with a Turkish doctor, she would need to speak Turkish. She had tried to find a Syrian doctor to work with but she hadn't succeeded. She had tried to find work with a Syrian organisation, but they were all part of the opposition and Susan had criticisms of the opposition and kept her distance from the internal divisions. She started to hate everyone: she hated the opposition after at first hating those loyal to the regime. In the end she agreed to do office work that any girl could have done, even one who hadn't graduated from secondary school. She accepted that in order to pay the rent. In Istanbul accommodation was expensive by Syrian standards, maybe four or five times higher.

Trying to understand what's happening to Syrians today is like studying for secondary school certificate: you feel dizzy, have headaches, want to vomit, feel confused and tense.

That's at the human level. Politically and militarily, I gave up trying to understand years ago.

I try to draw a map, as I learnt to do at university or at work. A map in which I show people's new places. But the map keeps changing.

My sister on the phone stops her daily soap opera and, just like every time, suddenly remembers. "I forgot to ask. How are you?"

Susan doesn't wait for me to answer because she thinks I'm living in the lap of luxury, in France, and that people are dying on land and at sea for a half or a quarter of what I have. I stopped talking to Susan about my situation months ago, and as soon as she asks her question, I know that the conversation is drawing to a close and she's asking the question only out of a sense of duty. So all I say is, "I'm fine."

I wrap up my conversation with Susan and then I call Samir in Holland. Samir is chirping with pleasure: "Today I had my last interview with the asylum department and I expect to get residence soon," he says.

Samir paints a rosy future for himself: "Tomorrow I'll get a residence permit and they'll give me a beautiful house in Amsterdam that's just right, and you can come to join us. I know you're feeling lonely and homesick. You'll be better off with us."

We move on to talk about our mother. I feel that our plans are taking us away from her. She's alone in Aleppo. We are looking forward to a better life in Europe, especially Susan and Samir I mean. I haven't made up my mind yet, and I don't want to go to France or any Western or Arab country. I want Aleppo.

Samir says: "That's her luck. It's war, sister. I'll try to get her to Holland after we have the residence permits. You know the fact that I have my wife and the children with me shortens the family reunification process. I'll try to persuade Mother to leave Aleppo."

I laugh bitterly. I know Mother will refuse to leave Aleppo though I don't understand why she's so attached to the city now that Father is dead and her three children have left.

Samir followed in Susan's footsteps and married early. In fact he went even further. He got married after graduating from secondary school. He told Father that since he was the only son he wasn't required to do military service and that he didn't need to continue his education after secondary school because he was going to work with Father since he was the only son, and so he didn't need any qualifications.

Samir didn't like working in a pharmacy and dealing with medicines. He liked drawing. He hadn't done well at school so he chose a short cut: working with Father. His aim in all this was a quick marriage with Jamila, whose family were planning to marry her off to one of her cousins.

Jamila was Samir's first love. She lived next door to us in the building. She played with us when she was young, before school age. Then she went to the same primary school as Samir. They used to go to school together and come back together. They were separated at middle school but he used to walk her to her school and they would come back together. Jamila's mother would say to Samir, "Look after her. You're like her brother. Jamila's your sister, just like Susan and Sara."

Samir and Jamila took me by surprise with their silent love. They didn't show that passion that's not hard to find among teenagers. They treated each other as friends or as brother and sister. Then Samir came to his father one day and started talking about marriage in general. When mother heard what he was saying she was delighted and she liked his point of view. She thought she would look for a bride for him but he cut her short. "Don't trouble yourself, Mother," he said, "Jamila lives upstairs. There's just one floor between us. Why look further?"

Susan and Samir both married before me, their elder sister, and had children. In fact they each married the first person they fell in love with. Their lives were simple and uncomplicated. Only I am the difficult one. I've never been attracted to a man and none of the marriage proposals I've received have appealed to me.

I was naïve and maybe I still am. I imagine that human beings are brothers. Women and men are brothers and sisters. I spent my childhood with Lorca, Samir and Majid and in the company of Susan and Jamila. I didn't distinguish between Samir or Lorca or Majid. I felt that they were all my brothers. I was surprised how different feelings developed between Samir and Jamila, and between Susan and Lorca. Once, after Jamila and Samir were engaged, Majid's mother said to my mother, "Why don't we marry Sara off to Majid?" I suddenly felt sick and my heart pounded in fear. "But Majid's like my brother!" I shouted as if possessed. "You say the same thing about all men, that they're all your brothers," my mother snapped back immediately.

I was puzzled and surprised by what my mother said. "It's not up to me," I said to myself. "What can I do? That's how I feel towards everyone I know and meet. They're all like Samir and Lorca and Majid. They're all my brothers."

I thought the world was made up of brothers and sisters and that by chance a brother and a sister would choose to live together, and then they would fetch children from somewhere.

My mother and father seemed like brother and sister to me. I never felt there was anything between them that was like what we see in Arabic films – whispers, caresses, kisses, smiles and seductions. I never saw my mother changing her clothes in front of my father, and she didn't treat him any differently from the way she treated us. So when mother would sometimes sing, when she forgot herself and was engrossed in housework, I imagined her talking to someone else, someone invisible, or that she was talking about some man far away.

When I went into my parents' bedroom when they were there, I usually saw my mother with her back turned on my father, even when she was talking, as though she were talking to some man who lived in some country far away. This was my game before going to bed in my early adolescence. Then my game developed and I had an imaginary man who lived in some country far away. I spoke to him every night and dozed off in the middle of a story in which I was rocking like a child. Instead of being rocked to sleep by my mother's stories, I was rocked to sleep by my stories about a man far away, whose name changed every night. I knew he was waiting for me somewhere, this man, and he was the only man I didn't feel was like a brother.

My conversation with Samir ended. I had missed half of it or more as I scribbled on my piece of paper and thought about things other than what Samir was saying and what I was scribbling. It was like suddenly waking up. That often happens to me in the metro: I come to my senses at the station where I'm getting off, as if I've been asleep at the other stations. My mind drifts off, usually to Aleppo. I found I had been unconsciously drawing what looks like a map of my Aleppo metro.

Did Hafal unconsciously inspire me to draw the map, or had I always wanted to design a metro in Aleppo like the Paris one?

I felt that the Paris metro was almost the city's umbilical cord. Paris kept its children in contact with each other through this cord. Which Parisians don't take the metro at least once in their lives? That would be almost impossible.

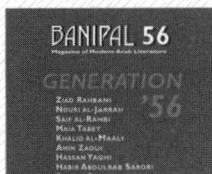

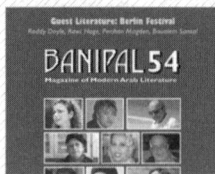

Paris brings all its children together, its biological children and its children by adoption, its coloured children of multiple shades of skin colour and multiple languages, multiple dialects, multiple religions and multiple ideologies.

I felt that the metro was the cord that fed Paris love and that the River Seine was its womb.

The map in front of me combined Paris lines and Aleppo lines.

I find I've drawn Line 1, the yellow line, starting from the Château de Vincennes. It continues to Châtelet, then rises towards Bab al-Hadid and passes through the old quarters of Aleppo until it reaches the Citadel.

Line 2, the blue line, comes out of Nation, and then proceeds until it reaches al-Kalassa by way of Bab Jenin and Souk al-Hal.

Line 3, the beige line, starts at Gallieni and ends at Saif al-Dawla.

Line 4, the red line, sets off from Porte d'Orléans and ends in al-Shahba al-Jadida, passing through Khaldiya, Nile Street and Mocambo.

Line 5, the orange line, goes from Place d'Italie, through Bustan Kull Ab, then turns on the hill and continues until the Latin Church.

My heart pounds as I read: Bustan Kull Ab. It seems strange to write it that way. I was always uncertain how it's written. I like writing it the way my father pronounced it when I was a child and as all the inhabitants of Aleppo pronounce it, as Bustan Kilab, or Bustan Kilayb in the Aleppan dialect. I always imagined it as a big garden full of dogs, as the name suggests in Arabic, and I was excited and keen to go and see that many dogs in one garden. But then I grew up and learnt my mistake. I looked it up in the Asadi encyclopaedia and realised that it meant the garden of Kul Ab, but I prefer to write it the way I learnt it: the Garden of Dogs.

I look at the map and smile happily because I've achieved a breakthrough. It's clear to me in the drawing that I've answered a question that I haven't consciously asked. If the Seine is the womb of Paris, what is the womb of Aleppo? The map shows that, just as the blue river surrounds most of the metro lines, it's the Citadel of Aleppo that connects most of the lines on my plan.

Translated from the author's novel *Metro Halab* (Aleppo Metro), published by Dar al-Tanweer, Beirut 2016

FAWAZ KADERI

Three Poems

TRANSLATED BY RAPHAEL COHEN

THE CHILD IS STILL

For Sari Ibrahim al-Saoud

The child is still
his eyes stare upwards
his fingers are perfect alone
his lips without a smile
his mouth full of shouts
his legs motionless and a thousand calls to play in the street.
The child is still
A woman shakes his head violently:
Get up my boy
The boy is still, unresponsive.
The stone he lies on moved
the ribs of the pavement moved
the universe trembled
a distant star sighed
and the killer smiled.
The child is still
his heart . . . ahh his heart.
A thin trickle of blood
a small hole in the body
opened by a not-stray bullet.

CHILD

This child, carried on shoulders,
looks from a crack at life,
at those walking in the funeral procession:
   the stones of the neighbourhood
   the trees, the birds, the dogs,
looks at the houses walking behind him
   the walls, the roofs, the schoolyard
and God follows, sad and broken
Heavens, rivers and white clouds
walking, too, behind him.
Only the Earth stays,
waiting for this angel, shivering from loneliness,
to return to her dust.

PANDEMONIUM

Thank you to the window
that from all this pandemonium
gave me something
to let me feel I'm still
alive and well in this madness
they call life.

HAITHAM HUSSEIN

Hostages of Memory

EXCERPTS FROM THE NOVEL,
TRANSLATED BY JONA FRAS

Chapter 3

Grandma Khatouna would break stale bread into pieces and put it into canvas bags to sell later. This was how she would remind herself of her past life, when she used to wander from village to village in the lands known as Jayaye Omriyan. There wasn't a single village she hadn't visited; and while she did come to know quite a few people in each of them, she never seemed to be able to settle down. She was always on the move, as if there was a crime pursuing her that she never could quite flee from, or a sin she hadn't received forgiveness for. She did, finally, come to settle down in Amouda, where she contented herself with a hut on the outskirts of town. Her children stayed with her, two boys barely a few years of age, and a black goat that was never tied up and during the night slept with them in the hut.

She was cautious towards everyone at the beginning. Whenever someone approached her house she would draw herself back, and ask sharply after their business before they could step closer. Gradually, once she had reassured herself that the locals only wanted to help her – to learn her story, do her a favour or two, perhaps discover some distant relation of hers – she came to trust them more. But she did not throw herself blindly into their trust. She ignored most of their offers, and would shut every door that might have been opened regarding the village she had come from, or her family or relatives. "From the broad lands of God," was all she had to say. Sometimes, she would be a little more specific, though only by repeating something everyone already knew: that she was from "above the line". And that, really, was the end of it.

People grew to accept this, and would no longer ask her – except occasionally. So she came known as Khatouna of Jayaye.

She experienced her share of calamity and misfortune during her first twenty-five years in the town. She would sew bedcovers and raise cows to provide for her little family. She also worked as midwife, and paid little attention to what she would sometimes hear from this or that woman whom she helped to deliver: that she was heartless, that she was never stirred by their screams or cries for help during labour – as if she hadn't delivered her two sons herself, or had never experienced the iron-melting pains of childbirth. She would comment only that it was her duty to do as she did, for the new mothers' sake. Labour wasn't a time to feel for others; it would only cause harm.

Her sons grew up working as delivery boys in the market. They both wore woollen skullcaps and prayed dutifully at the mosque every Friday. People came to like them, and as the years passed they would no longer ask them why they had come to Amouda, or any other of Grandma Khatouna's many secrets –

which looked as if she would take them to her grave, her soul never being re-lieved of the pain of keeping them hidden. She wouldn't disclose them to any-one, not even her boys, no matter how much they begged her to do so. She never told them even a single word more than what she told everyone else. So they were forced to accept her silence, and – like everyone else – stopped ask-ing her. Still, it gnawed at them, from time to time.

Sufi Alo reached and passed thirty without once broaching the subject of marriage with his mother, or his brother for that matter. He knew very well how pitiful their circumstances were, even as he and his brother advanced from being delivery boys to street peddlers to partners in a small store in the Arasa Market. But then there came the day when Sufi Farho told Alo to wait for him at the gate of the mosque after evening prayers, and asked him to marry his daughter.

The women called this daughter of Farho's "Shekrawka Karrik", meaning she was half-deaf. Sufi Farho's offer to Sufi Alo came on the basis of their shared religious devotion, and because Alo had proven his good nature and excellent morals, and also because Alo was a capable worker and Farho wouldn't have to worry about his daughter if she were married to him. He hastened to add that he would, of course, help Alo cover some of the wedding expenses. He wouldn't ask for a bride price either; Alo upholding his promise and taking care of his daughter would be bride price enough.

Alo, more than a little stunned, accepted Farho's offer there and then. He swore he would never turn his eyes away from Farho's daughter, and never let her want for anything. He did not care if his betrothed was old or deaf, or that Sufi Farho may have approached him as a last resort for a daughter, whose hand had never been asked for and who had lost all hope of marrying. For Alo, to become a son-in-law to someone like Farho had never been anything more than a distant dream – and yet, here he was now, on the verge of this dream becoming reality.

They both had supernatural explanations ready to account for their good fortune. Alo liked to think it was God's own unadulterated love that chose him from among so many others. Outwardly, Farho ascribed it to fate, keeping to himself the true reasons that had forced him to make his proposal.

But the new groom did not care to look for these reasons; nor did Grandma Khatouna. The marriage was the right way forward. This they knew, or at least convinced themselves.

Chapter 4

After Sufi Farho had made Alo burst with joy over tidings he had never dared to dream of hearing, he added a comment. Just a small one; but he was obliged to mention it, he said. His daughter had a "hearing problem".

Alo didn't quite know how to respond to Sufi Farho's overflowing generosity, and his sincerity embarrassed him. He had little to say other than that, of course, he did not attach any sort of importance to the issue of hearing problems. And so it was – even later on, when the "hearing problem" really turned out to be almost complete deafness, one for which no amount of shouting did any good. You had to use hand gestures, or yell loudly enough that all the neighbours would hear.

But Alo was happy to live a quiet life, without all the likely annoyances his wife might have brought him from gossip and prattling. And so was she. Her deafness, and her father's cruelty, had imposed a total silence upon her life. She lived isolated from everything, her world confined to the demands of housework and motherhood. As for her conjugal duties, they soon virtually disappeared; she got used to ignoring and suppressing her own desires, like most other women she knew, and only responded to those of her husband, even as these grew less and less frequent as time went on.

She had lost her hearing more than twenty years before, when she was still a child. She was sweeping the front doorway on a summer evening, a little before sunset, with a bit of water splashed on the ground so she would not raise dust – when she suddenly caught sight her father, marching swiftly towards home, returning early from the market. Farho was shouting and cursing at her, and when he came near he punched her so strongly she fell down and hit her head on the wall behind her. He ordered her to get inside the house, with another stream of curses, and swore by God that he would murder her if he saw her sweeping the front doorway ever again.

This monstrous behaviour of Sufi Farho's has another story behind it, which can be told here in brief. When he was in the market that day after the afternoon prayers, he happened to overhear a conversation among a group of delivery boys – whom he would later describe as filthy and depraved – sipping their tea and exchanging whispered remarks about the guiles and artifices of women.

These were young men well-versed in sowing mistrust and spinning tales

that revealed people to be malicious and wicked, even if they appeared innocent. A girl might, for example, use the excuse of sweeping the front doorway
in order to be outside at a particular time agreed with her boyfriend. She would
take her time sweeping and standing there until her friend came by and saw
her or spoke to her in order to arrange another meeting; this would, later on,
lead to disaster and tragedy, when the two met somewhere far from people's
eyes, and the man would take what he wanted from her, and then cast her aside
like a wet rag . . .

Before Sufi Farho could fully absorb the devastating shock waves of what he
had just heard, another of the delivery boys interjected that one should get rid
of such a girl immediately by marrying her off as soon as the "sieve passes between her legs", that is as soon as she matures. "Wean her off the tit and find
her something harder to suck on," he added, to general laughter; it was more
than clear what he was referring to.

These warnings echoed in Farho Tawtus's ears, and doubt began to creep
over him. He hadn't been able to find a match for his daughter, and so, slowly,

Introduction to *Hostages of Memory*

The novel was initially published in Syria in 2009, has been translated
into Czech (2016), and is currently being translated into French. It
chronicles the story of a Kurdish woman, Khatouna, and her two sons,
Alo and Ahme, as they move through villages in the Turkish-Syrian border-
lands in the 1960s, fleeing from the consequences of an event in Khatouna's
past which she stubbornly keeps secret. The family comes to settle in the town
of Amouda, in Syria, and though viewed suspiciously by the locals at first,
Khatouna and her boys manage to build a life for themselves, lifting themselves from extreme poverty into something resembling a dignified existence.
A series of family fortunes and misfortunes follows, during which the reader
finally comes to learn the truth regarding the crime which forced Khatouna
to flee her home and become a refugee in her own land.

Through its Kurdish characters, *Hostages of Memory* offers the reader a unique
glimpse into the extremely complex social fabric of North-Eastern Syria, and
issues of identity and history woven through life in this borderland region. It
is also, however, a novel about family; the importance of blood ties in the face
of adversity; and a subtle mystery which draws the reader to find out why, precisely, Khatouna and her boys would come to live as they did.

his suspicions grew. They're right, he told himself. They have to be.

He rushed home for sunset prayer, aching to empty his bladder but forced to wait until after prayer unless he wanted to invalidate the ablutions he had taken such pains to perform earlier that day. When he spotted his daughter sweeping the front doorway of the house without a veil on, he was immediately convinced the delivery boys had spoken the truth. Rage and jealousy overcame him, and so he did what he did. While his daughter still considered herself a child, her father and everyone else regarded girls of her age as already quite mature, with honour that had to be protected. So she became a victim of her own naïve good opinion of herself – or rather, the mistrust of her father. She was considered mature, and on this basis was she judged.

The incident rescued those around her from the tumult she would likely have caused, and rescued her from the tumult that would have been caused by those around her. Farho, however, would never again be at peace, and would never stop asking God's forgiveness for his suspicions about his daughter. He tried to atone for his actions by spoiling her, by being nice to her, by speaking to her gently and sparing her work and generally asking less from her. And yet she was punished if she spoke up, and left in pain if she remained silent. She was only ever happy when she was doing housework. She remained scrupulous and reliable in all she did, and kept her honour intact.

But Farho's punch had already damaged her inexorably in other ways. Suspicions swirled around her, also malicious gossip that only cared for what it wanted to find, no matter how convincing other answers might have been. Farho chastised himself over and over again for using violence when he shouldn't have. Still, his madness and rashness and blind jealousy had kindled the fire, and no amount of remorse on his part could put it out. The genie of speculation and slander was out of its bottle; and, as the proverb says, vicious tongues are hardly a belt that one can tighten or loosen whenever one wants.

Translated from the author's novel *Rahain al-Khatia'a* (Hostages of Sin),
published by Dar al-Takween, Damascus 2009

ROSA YASSIN HASSAN

People under a Spell

EXCERPT FROM THE NOVEL

TRANSLATED BY WILLIAM M HUTCHINS

Al-Lujat and its Story-Sated Plain

On that day when angry noises drew me out onto the terrace of my house, which I built to face the Hauran plain that had captivated me with its majesty, Al-Lujat seemed to spread before me: a mountain as wavy as a sea of heaving basalt.

Dududuummm . . . dududummmm: muffled roaring sounds like distant explosions! I was hearing this for the first time in a place where calm usually prevailed. I was shocked to see columns of dark smoke rise from the area of Basr al-Harir, a town situated opposite my village but separated from it by kilometres of the fertile agricultural lands of Al-Lujat. One wide asphalt road headed like a patient camel drover toward the towns of Izra and al-Shaykh Miskin after splitting Busr al-Harir in two.

The usually intense, blistering heat of summer might have caused a person to imagine he saw a mirage of vapor rising from the boulders that clustered together as far as the eye could see; but this was December 2011, and the stinging cold made it hard even to stand upright. Those columns of smoke were definitely not caused by hot weather—far from it! I realized that Busr al-Harir was being shelled before my eyes! I could not believe it! During the past months, while I sat reading or writing in my study, I had heard bursts of gunfire from Busr al-Harir. The empty expanse between our two villages was normally a silent, rock-rimmed void and magnified the sound of the gunfire. Occasionally I would hear a Doshka heavy machine gun being fired, usually from the back of a pickup truck. Security officers used them to break up the demonstrations that had begun to flare up there. When those demonstrations were held at night and silence dominated the void, I could hear, in my house—like

the whispers of wandering spirits—young people chanting and, occasionally, shouting "Allahu Akbar". These clashes had recently become increasingly violent, and it seemed that the revolutionaries had introduced new weapons. Cries of "Allahu Akbar" now dominated the ever louder voices, especially once shots started to ring out. These boisterous young people reminded me of the Red Bolshevik revolutionaries who once shouted "Hurrraaaaaah"—a cry that instilled rebellious force in tired bodies. Such calls have become de facto talismans for revolution. I did not feel they referred to Islam at all when they shouted "Allahu Akbar"—at least not at first.

But with time all that changed.

I realized I was screaming to my wife, Siham. My screams had clearly been hysterical enough that, in the middle of December, she came outside with wet hair, wrapped in her bathrobe. Her eyes revealed her alarm. She stood motionless beside me, staring at the distant columns of smoke as they ascended.

"They're shelling Busr al-Harir!"

A new sound boomed out, and a dark cloud appeared in its wake.

"Those dogs . . ." Seconds later I remembered my friend Dr Nafi' al-Hariri. What had happened to him? Had the shells hit his house? His clinic? A member of his family? Questions shook my head and heart.

Standing beside me, Siham began to weep; I was almost going crazy because I didn't know what I could possibly do. I impulsively started running towards the road, but Siham's shrieks brought me back: "Khalil! Khalil! Please! Where are you going?"

I rushed to the telephone in the house, because for many days cell phone service had been cut throughout the region. The telephone at his house and the one at his clinic were both dead. So they had cut landline service too. Dududuummm . . . the roar of a new bombardment stronger than the previous ones.

Siham took a seat, dried her tears, and trembled as she dressed beside the space heater. I didn't feel my normal desire to watch this fifty-five-year-old adolescent, who still hid her naked body from my gaze as she dressed, concealing features I had surreptitiously memorized. If I peeked or ventured a flirtatious remark, she would blush with embarrassment. I usually enjoyed watching her dress; but today I was almost non compos mentis. I had no idea what might have happened to Dr Nafi', especially since I understood that he had been targeted by the regime's forces for some time and that his clinic had become something like a field hospital for Busr al-Harir and the surrounding communities, to which the revolution had spread like an infection, one by one.

The last time he visited—when summer was in full bloom, about five months earlier—he had protested: "I won't leave my town now when it needs me the most!" He had parked his car at some distance from my house and then brought three young men with him in the dark of the night. One seemed weak and exhausted, and I sensed he leaned forward as he walked.

Dr Nafi' arrived with a black cloth bag and an affectionate smile that rarely left his lips.

"Khalil, my friend, I couldn't think of a safer place for Mahmoud to hide than your house. He was shot in the abdomen today. He's a youngster from the Movement and was participating in the demonstration with us. This is his brother Umar."

He drew back the jacket of the young man, whose face became even paler. A dark stain circled his midriff.

"Khalil, they're using exploding bullets! Just one burns everything near it when it enters the body. May God protect him! I was able to remove the shrapnel at my house, but he needs care and rest."

"Of course . . . certainly. Gladly."

"You realize that with these continual, intrusive raids on the community no house there is safe. If they find an injured man, they take him."

"Of course . . . certainly, Doctor. Consider this house his home."

I was less certain than I claimed, because my neighbors had been watching our house closely for months. Although my neighbors were actually my relatives, they wouldn't hesitate to tell the security men about any stranger who came to my house from the south. What if they discovered he was a wounded revolutionary from Daraa? I was thinking I could hide him in the pantry, since it was shielded from sight by the kitchen. Then I considered taking him by car to Suwayda, which was a few kilometres away, because that at least was a city where he could disappear. But there were roadblocks on that road, and he would be arrested merely because he came from a city associated with the Movement. So I immediately dismissed that notion.

Dr Nafi' may have gleaned my reservations from the look in my eyes; he said, "If there's any problem, Khalil, I can . . ."

I interrupted and reassured him.

"Today they stormed the village at dawn. Fifty buses full of armed security agents—as if they were heading to a war, Man. They detained more than a hundred young men. The situation has become unbearable, Khalil. Unbearable!"

* * *

The brothers Mahmoud and Umar Youssef were in an unenviable situation. Khalil Abu al-'Azm could hardly refuse to shelter and hide two revolutionaries from the Movement, and not merely because he felt sorry for them. In fact, he supported the revolution with his whole being and felt utterly powerless to influence the course of events. Moreover, he wished to banish some of the shame he felt because of his extended family's pro-government stance as well as his sect's. So he brushed aside any possible consequences of his generosity and felt happy.

Dr Nafi' al-Hariri placed a hand on the shoulder of the third young man, who sat beside Umar Youssef, patting it fondly. The youth's body was scrawny, and his bones showed through his faded t-shirt.

"Our friend Muhaymid Abu al-Dud has also been active in the demonstrations." Then he laughed.

"From Busr al-Harir too?"

"No, Muhaymid is from Daraa al-Balad. He came to Busr a few weeks ago."

Muhaymid Abu al-Dud, who seemed embarrassed, smiled at the arrangements Dr Nafi' was making.

The physician explained that the nickname "Abu al-Dud" or "Worm Dad" had clung to Muhaymid since childhood and referred in some way to his socio-economic status. Since childhood he had been a concrete and construction worker, carrying pumice stone in Daraa al-Balad. In the past few months, though, Abu al-Dud had become one of the most renowned organizers there. He was one of the coordinators of the demonstrations. He made the rounds on his Vespa scooter to inform people in the area of the time of the next demonstration, knocking on every door he passed and whispering "Today at eight" to the person who answered. He completed his mission conscientiously.

"We stopped using cell phones some time ago. They keep us under surveillance all the time, and on many occasions wireless service is interrupted."

Muhaymid Abu al-Dud's voice was hoarse, and his eyes glinted with pride as he apologized for his hoarseness, citing the action-packed demonstration of the previous day. So he did not merely schedule demonstrations; he actually led them and shouted the slogans. Being so scrawny allowed him to ride on the shoulders of other demonstrators. He was most often seen on their shoulders raising his fist in the air.

For some reason Khalil Abu al-'Azm asked him: "Muhammad, why do you demonstrate?"

Even though he referred to the young man by his real name rather than its diminutive, his words or his languid, patronizing tone evidently betrayed him. Abu al-Dud was upset and exploded: "You intellectuls—and the Syrian regime with you—think that I and people like me are scum."

"God forbid! Not at all!"

Even so, he persisted, "No . . . I get it . . . You naturally think I'm scum. I don't demonstrate because I want democracy or what you call a civil society. I know nothing about democracy or civility. I've only heard about them since the revolution. I know just one thing; I know I feel my own worth now. That's something I never felt before. When I ride on people's shoulders, I feel I am a man. I shout for liberty and honor. Demonstrations are the only place where I feel my humanity. That's why I won't return home, even if I end up being martyred. By the way, many of the other young men are like me."

His eyes flaming with fury, Muhaymid walked outside to wait for the physician.

"Sorry if he took my question the wrong way . . . I . . ."

"Not your fault, Khalil. Abu al-Dud is very sensitive about his class background." Dr Nafi' laughed. "As you intellectuals put it." He laughed out loud once more.

Khalil Abu al-'Azm thought he would write an article about this Muhaymid Abu al-Dud. In it he would mention the young man's class origins but then say that the Syrian revolution belonged to all classes and was not only for one level of society. It was a socio-political revolution—a vertical, not a horizontal one. He brooded about what Dr Nafi' had suggested.

Khalil Abu al-'Azm, however, would never learn what happened to Muhaymid Abu al-Dud after that visit. His skinny, scrawny figure, which poverty had fashioned, was transformed when he picked up the new Kalashnikov a close friend gave him. That cruel rifle seemed to belie Muhaymid's charm and his diminutive figure but drew him into its world, granting him a look of distinction. In seconds it provided him with gravitas. He felt this pulse through his very cells; he was now an influential person of obvious worth. At least that was what he sensed with his entire being. From that day forth, Muhaymid ceased organizing demonstrations; he clung to his assault rifle until the day he was killed in a battle in Al-Lujat.

The cloth bag was filled with gauze, bandages, disinfectant, and anti-inflammatory medicine. Dr al-Nafi' handed them to Khalil, uttering a few terse sentences about their use. He left behind the scent of anxiety, a heavy burden, and a flood of questions Khalil could not answer. Umar Youssef and Muhaymid Abu al-Dud departed with him.

At the door, Dr Nafi whispered anxiously: "The situation is no longer tenable, Khalil. The young men have begun to think seriously of armed struggle. The rusty rifles we have aren't adequate any more. The regime attacks the town almost daily as well as the surrounding ones. Young men are killed every day. They are arrested every day. The situation is intolerable, man."

"Armed struggle?"

"Yes. Armed struggle. What else can we do, Khalil? Should we huddle in our homes like dogs—worse off than we used to be? If we wish to persevere, we must take up arms."

". . . ."

"The regime can hardly believe that this city, which was always close to it and obedient, would rebel and then revolt against it so suddenly."

". . . ."

"My friend, each person must decide for himself, but the decision will be almost unanimous. How many months of almost daily killings can a community accept? So, my friend, don't be angry at me; this is the only way for us to repel the Shabiha militia and the security forces."

"But, this shouldn't mean we kill them the way they kill us."

"There's no other option . . . If you know of one, tell me."

"Armed combat, my friend, will move matters to another plateau—one we do not control, one that isn't appropriate for us, one with untold consequences."

Dr Nafi' bade me farewell that night after hugging me. I sensed then that, despite his fond smile, his spirit had already parted from me. He left me with my burden, questions, and fear of future events. My turmoil was too personal for me to confide to anyone except my brother, Umran Abu-'Azm. He was the only person who could understand me. Umran was tired, though—tired to the point of exhaustion—and I could not lay any more burdens based on my anxiety on him.

Then the summer of 2011 arrived, and the revolutionaries transitioned from facing the regime with angry voices to using machine guns and angry bullets.

And that was months ago!

The roar of today's shelling made me think back to that night.

Mahmoud Youssef had hidden with me till his wounds were almost healed. Siham devised the solution of putting him in the cellar, where no curious person could intrude. She moved the little TV she used in the kitchen to the basement, where she placed it opposite the young man to keep him from growing bored while he lay still for long periods. I told him: "By the way, this is a big sacrifice on her part. She has given up her kitchen TV for you." Mahmoud blushed and smiled.

I spent the following weeks reading beside him by the light of the dangling light. Piled near us were sacks of the supplies I collected here for the revolutionaries to transport to regions that needed them. We referred to them as food baskets. There were also sacks of medical supplies: adhesive strips, bandages, needles for tetanus vaccines, gauze, and cotton swabs. My nostrils were filled with the smell of olives and rancid bulgar and tahini, and my head was filled with Mahmoud's stories about what was happening in towns and villages of Daraa. It seemed clear that the young men of the opposition had decided to take a different path from his revolution. They were frantically arming themselves, and Al-Lujat was the womb that expanded to embrace their nascent dream.

Mahmoud's health continued to improve little by little, and after eight days he was able to move around the room. In five more days he could speak fluently and laugh. His laughter tickled me, and I felt he was almost like my own son. His brother, Umar Youssef, had come to visit him only twice. The first time he was accompanied by a stranger from the village of Tafas; I never learned his name. When he shook my hand, I noticed that his palm was rough and his grip strong and firm. His head was wrapped in a faded cloth, and his gallabiya was the same color. The two brothers whispered to each other in the room for a long time while I stayed with the stranger in the sitting room. He was silent, and I didn't know how to initiate a conversation with him! I welcomed him to my home again, and he nodded his head resolutely. Siham brought in the brass coffeepot and offered him a cup of Arab coffee. To avoid looking at her, he bowed his head till she left the room. Then he savored the coffee with delight. He said it was the best coffee he had ever tasted and fell silent. After some awkward minutes I asked about their situation.

Then, before returning to his silence, he volunteered a number of terse sentences: "Look, Brother, I had three sons. Since the siege of Daraa began last March I have dedicated them to freedom. That day I came to the large demonstration with my three young men, I had written on the belly of each his name and that he was from Tafas. Then if one was martyred, good people would know where he came from and what his name was. Their names remained written on their bellies till that night. The middle boy was martyred in the demonstration in Daraa al-Balad. Praise God for granting him martyrdom. The other two survived . . . two boys I have dedicated . . . to freedom, and only God knows whether He will protect them."

My tongue struggled and I stammered, wishing to respond to what he had said. I couldn't. Language betrayed me just when I needed it most. Umar rescued me by joining us. They departed. I never saw that man from Tafas again, but he will haunt my memory as long as I live!

The second time Umar Youssef came alone. I sensed later that he had come to bid his brother farewell, because Mahmoud's eyes were red when I returned to his room. Umar was sniffling when he left and turned his face away from me. He departed without ever returning to us. Later I learned that he would be forced to remain in Damascus, the capital. It seemed that his name had been sought at the checkpoints and that he had to do many things in Damascus; that's what Mahmoud told me.

* * *

Khalil Abu al-'Azm had no idea what Mahmoud and his brother discussed that night. Umar bade his brother farewell without knowing when he might be destined to see him again. He needed to hide in Damascus and maintain his ties to friends in the security services, but that was a task comparable to hopping on one foot along the edge of an abyss. His mission was to stay up to date on secret plans known only inside the walls of the security apparatus and then to share these with the revolutionaries and activists of al-Ghouta.

"I have this special competence that is valuable to the revolution," he told his brother before departing. "I'm the only person who can perform this task skilfully; someone who has this opportunity can achieve a lot," he added.

"But, Brother. This is a dangerous game."

His brother nodded silently.

Khalil Abu al-'Azm, though, heard none of this final conversation between them.

A few months earlier Umar Youssef learned about a fax sent to the office of the head of the branch with which he enjoyed good relations. This paper was stamped "Top Secret" at the top, meaning that the only person authorized to view this document was the head of the branch. Orders from the highest command decreed that 3,000 shots should be fired into the air every night near the city of Jaramana to increase fears of residents there that terrorist bands were infiltrating from al-Ghouta. Then citizens would feel increasingly dependent on the regime.

"But that was months ago . . . at the outset of the revolution," Mahmoud Youssef told Khalil Abu al-'Azm, a day before saying farewell to him. Khalil immediately thought of a phrase Hitler had once used: "If you want to control a people, convince them that they are in danger and that their safety is threatened."

"Mr. Khalil, they know that in Jaramana, and are ready for all sorts of malicious plots."

"Thank you. Take good care of yourself and if you speak to your brother, tell him to take care of himself too. It's dangerous to play with brutes!"

"Don't worry about us. We're from Daraa and fear nothing. We were the first to tear down a statue of Hafez al-Assad with our bare hands—in the first month of the revolution! Do you think we'll be afraid?"

Then Khalil asked him to recount how the statue was toppled. He was keen to learn all about that. Mahmoud did not hesitate to describe the event in full detail from the start of the demonstration to their discovery that the statue could be easily demolished once its skin was punctured.

That evening hundreds of conflicting thoughts bounced around in Khalil Abu al-'Azm's head as he sat opposite Mahmoud Youssef, who lay in his bed in the cellar. Khalil held a book about folklore and legends by Sayyid Mahmoud al-Qemany. It lay open on his lap for an hour, without his turning a page—without his even seeing the words. His consciousness was full of his thoughts, which were tormenting him as they struggled inside his mind. Mahmoud interrupted these thoughts when he suddenly remarked: "Once Umar learned that a booby-trapped vehicle would explode somewhere in al-Ghouta—I no longer remember where. It was set to explode during the funeral there of a martyr. So he alerted the young men, and the funeral cortège did not take to the streets. And the car did not explode!"

"What happened then?"

"Apparently he started to suspect that they suspected him."

"What can he do?"

"He's going to be a lot more careful about what he does. That's why he won't be able to come here any more!"

". . . ."

"Mr. Khalil, what good are all these books you read? The only books I've ever read were schoolbooks!"

Siham, who had diligently brought food to us in the basement room during Mahmoud's stay there, brought us what would be our last supper together. She exchanged a few words with us and departed, leaving us to a prolonged discussion. I was eager to learn more about that little known area of my country, one that had become more mysterious and troubled since the flame of revolution was ignited. Listening to him, I realized how little I knew. Mahmoud's questions also revealed how little he knew about our area, even though only a few kilometres separated our communities.

"High, deep and invisible walls appear to separate Suwayda from Daraa!"

He did not seem to get what I meant.

"Like the walls that isolate most regions of Syria from each other!"

He still did not respond; instead he started to discuss stories that had begun to rise like sand dunes in Daraa and the surrounding region during the last few months. The tales began on March 18, 2011, and were still flowing. Toward the end of the evening, when Mahmoud was flipping channels on the small TV opposite him and I was reading *What is Globalization* by Ulrich Beck, he suddenly laughed out loud. He chortled and guffawed till tears came to his eyes. I started laughing along with him without any idea what the joke was. He had stopped changing channels at the official government station and was watching the confession of a dishevelled young man clad in navy blue pyjamas. The gist of his confession was that he belonged to an armed terrorist group.

Mahmoud shouted: "That's Abu al-Samar . . . our village drunk. They arrested him on the outskirts of Daraa about a month ago."

The youth on television was saying that he had gone to Saudi Arabia and received money from a person there—three hundred thousand Syrian lira—to use to overthrow the regime here. Mahmoud laughed even louder. "Saudi Arabia? Abu al-Samar never left the village. Saudi Arabia, Abu al-Samar?"

* * *

I never saw Dr Nafi' al-Hariri again. I heard he was arrested one night in an ambush on the heights of Al-Lujat. One of my contacts told me he had left the country and fled to Jordan. A young man wearing a red keffiyah and torn jeans, though, told me quickly—while loading six bags of food supplies into his three-wheeled truck—that Dr Nafi' had been kidnaped by a Shabiha militia from Suwayda. Then he lowered his gaze, perhaps conscious of the look of shame in my eyes.

"How do you know?"

"My cousin saw them. They were patrolling near here."

"May God protect him wherever he is."

"Sorry, Mr. Khalil; I didn't mean to imply anything. Don't take any more burdens on yourself, Sir. We cherish your efforts and those of honorable people like you."

"Uncle, don't mention it. This is our duty. May God protect all of you."

Before he drove off swiftly in his tartira, he turned toward me and said, "If all the Druze were like you, Mr. Khalil, and like your friends, we would have toppled the regime long ago."

He vanished as quickly as he had arrived, and I never saw him again.

With the passing days I actually felt ever more distant from the people of Al-Lujat. The revolution set off on another course, remote from me! Weapons dominated the conflict, and extremism became increasingly prevalent as the death toll rose. This was not the revolution I had dreamt of. I had wanted a luminous revolution to oppose the regime's dark tyranny. Obviously what I wanted did not occur.

Some days later another young man came to collect the sacks of supplies I

hid in the basement room where Mahmoud Youssef had spent his convales-
cence. When I asked him about the young man with the red keffiyah and ripped
jeans—the one who drove the three-wheeled truck—he told me he had been
martyred. He had fallen in the past Friday's demonstration, shot in the head.
In fact, his brain spilled out on the asphalt, and he died at once. The youth re-
ported this as calmly as if he had been saying "Good morning" to a neighbor.
He tossed the last word at me as he threw the last bag of supplies into the car
boot and then drove away. When I came to my senses and wanted to ask him
about Dr Nafi' al-Hariri, the roaring sound of the departing automobile
drowned out everything.

* * *

Today, without any warning, someone knocked on the door. No one had
done that for many weeks.

Siham tried to suppress her sobs as she quickly finished dressing. The knocks
did not seem to suggest anything dangerous, but Khalil shivered as he walked
the few meters to the door. He trembled from rage, fear, frustration, and anxiety. Busr al-Harir was still being shelled, and the atmosphere in his house was
lethal, desperate.

Abu Mithqal, Khalil Abu al-'Azm's neighbor and cousin, was at the door.

"May God strengthen them and grant them good health. May God strengthen
the army . . ."

He said this quite seriously as he left his sandals at the door and entered the
parlor. When Khalil did not respond, Abu Mithqal declared: "By God, they
will, God willing, rid the country of the terrorists and armed gangs and rescue
us. We've been too afraid to sleep for months. By God, all this time I've been
thinking the terrorists would attack us, plunder our possessions, and slaughter
us in our beds."

"What terrorists?" Khalil asked, breaking his silence while Siham attempted
to signal him to keep still. Abu Mithqal's face looked even more anxious.

"The villains!"

"Who are the villains?"

"The armed gangs!"

"Who are the armed gangs?"

"Brother, what's wrong with you? The gangs are the guys destroying the
country, spreading chaos, and killing our young men. There are now dozens
of martyrs from our areas: Zayn al-Din, Abu Turaba, al-Khidir, Zaydan, to name
just a few. All of them died as martyrs in Daraa and Homs. Who killed them?"

"Your regime killed them by drafting them to fight in its war."

"What do you mean, Brother? Young men serve in the army to defend the fatherland."

"Who told you so?"

"Everyone says that. The satellite channels do, the political commentators, His Excellency the President discussed them in his address . . . and . . ."

"God damn you and your president," Khalil shouted. Abu Mithqal's face turned as white as the wall behind him.

"So, Brother, don't you see they beat up people . . . those are people, houses, men, children, and women. They're all terrorists!"

" . . . ."

"Brother, Khalil, I'm talking about the armed terrorists—not about the inhabitants of Busr al-Harir."

"What houses are being shelled, Brother? Do they belong to terrorists or to the residents of Busr?"

"The men shelling them are the armed gangs."

"Why don't the armed gangs shell you?"

"Because the army and security forces protect us."

"Why don't the army and security forces protect the people in Busr too?"

" . . . ."

"Brother, you need to wake up. You should all wake up. Your whole life, you've bought from them and they've bought from you. You've sold to them and they've sold to you. All your lives you have been neighbors. What's changed? What's come over you? Tell me."

" . . . ."

Even though he was yelling at Abu Mithqal, Khalil felt sorry for his cousin who was acting like a child being scolded by his mother. He looked pale, anxious, fearful, and agitated. He started staring at Siham, whose cheeks were flushed from shame and embarrassment. Abu Mithqal muttered a few incomprehensible words.

All the same, Khalil's anger had not cooled. He knew very well that the men of his family had been whispering behind his back. They were suspicious about his covert transactions, his defence of the people of Daraa, and his possible assistance for them, despite their lack of knowledge of any incriminating evidence. With his words he was severing the last thread that could possibly provide him any cover here. Even while shouting at Abu Mithqal he realized how extraordinarily difficult it would be to remain in his house after this.

Abu Mithqal stammered, slipped on his sandals, and then swiftly and furiously left Khalil Abu al-'Azm's parlor, where the latter was already asking his wife to begin packing her bags, since this was no longer any place for them.

They would lock up the house and move to Damascus.

"My brother Umran told me there's an empty apartment over the cafeteria he runs in Jaramana. He'll rent that to us once matters calm down. I have an agreement with him about that. By God, darling, let's hurry. I can't stay here a second longer."

Translated from *Al-Lathina Massahum Sihr* (People under a Spell),
published by Manshoorat al-Jamal, Beirut 2016

People under a Spell

This is a tale of Syria between 2011 and 2013, a time when the Syrian revolution started to transform itself into a fully-fledged civil war. The narrative, however, takes us back to a period long before that time frame in an attempt to identify the revolution's root causes and to find answers to such compelling questions as why Syrian society collapsed almost completely in such a short period, and why the secular democratic groups as well as the moderate religious currents have retreated in the face of rising waves of extremism, hatred, and violence.

While the major theme is a national political crisis, the novel is built around tales of ordinary people. It monitors the tiny details of their daily lives, and foregrounds their internal desires and emotions, and shows how they changed over time. The aim is to use those narratives to build a panoramic picture of the full spectrum of Syrian society.

The narrative is structured around characters from different opposing factions and groups, fragmented along political, religious, sectarian, racial or ethnic lines. The novel attempts to monitor those differences, which escalate sometimes into class-based and cultural conflicts. Combining reality and fiction, the novel uses "polyphony" as its underlying technique, with narrative rotating between an "omniscient" narrator and different characters who share their individual accounts and personal experiences. It also uses the technique of jumping between different times, and making sudden shifts between places and dates, which brings it closer to the boundaries of a "fragmented narrative". Other techniques employed include cinematic ellipsis, dialogue, and long monologues.

Rosa Yassin Hassan

NADA MENZALJI

A green window

POEM, TRANSLATED BY VALENTINA VIENE

I told you!
If I light up a cigarette I'll smoke the world.
It's not tobacco that I'm talking about.
It's my subtle way of saying
I am gifted enough to be addicted to you, too.
Precisely as I wanted it,
it was a warning sign,
more vague than it should be.
Adrenaline flooded profusely.

Those who rescued us
thought I was a mermaid,
the one who loved the prince
and sold her beautiful tail for legs.

And when they failed to recognise you
they assumed you had to be
"the handsomest drowned man in the world"*.

I wanted to remind you of the window,
that wooden green window
whose handle trapped
the sleeve of your broad smile.
Did you close it?
Or did you forget
and the shutters are still open?

I also forgot
to erase the kisses from the memories of the rooms,

those rooms that gossip
about what they saw
when they suffer from loneliness.

They wrecked the house
but the scene remained intact:
the man laughing
as he forgot to close the window,
the woman, counting the spoils on the mirror.
A little bite,
on the way to Everest,
where both sides left their fingerprints,
without writing their names
or the date.

* The Handsomest Drowned Man in the World is a short story by Gabriel García Márquez, written
  in 1968, with the English translation published in 2005.

NOURI AL-JARRAH

BOAT TO LESBOS

ELEGY TO THE DAUGHTERS OF NA'SH[1]

TRANSLATED BY CAMILO GOMEZ-RIVAS

I saw lightning in the east
in a wink
then west
I saw the sun dripping
in its blood
and the sea agitated
and the past robbed of its books.

GREEK TABLET

(The Call of Sappho)
I

Suffering Syrians, beautiful Syrians, Syrian brothers fleeing death. You won't
    reach the shores on rafts but will be born on beaches with the foam.
Lost gold dust you are, melted gold dust, scattered, dulled.
From abyss to abyss in the hollow of the sea of the Rum, with the star fish
    and her brother, the roving squid, the waves convey you under the light of
    Ursa Major, the Daughters of Na'sh.

• • •

Like mermaids born in the quivering light, beautiful Syrian women set
    tender, wounded soles on the rocks and grey sand of Lesbos.
Come down from the fruits of al-Sham
to the rocks of pain.

• • •

Brother Syrians, rolling on waves, killed on the beaches, feverish, gasping
on dark shores with morning-like faces, here, in Lesbos that Troy made
cry.
Come, let me kiss your cheeks, rosy with fear.

• • •

Come, friends. The sand of the shores gleaming in your eyes, the East
rippling golden ears of wheat in the copper of your faces. Rise as the high
mountains rose in your smooth cheeks. You swing in my mind as the
poplars swung in the wind of your days and the apple blossoms scattered
in the gale of your crossing. Come into the darkness of Lesbos, you
Syrians who emerged from the broken tablet of the alphabet.

• • •

Come down, be the blood of light and the alphabet of language.

• • •

How, my child, did you not make it into my arms? How did the wave ebb
away with you from me and leave you there on the shore of Izmir, an
angel without wings?
We carried in skins the best wine from Lattakia. The best wine. Grapes in
the boats of Cypriots, on the shoulders of sailors from Crete. Grapes
from al-Sham, from Darayya, Douma, and Wadi al-Shamiyyat, sweet balm
on their hands.
I sent my neighboring sisters carrying water. They took it to the beach and
returned with a boy they said was sleeping. When they laid him out on the
sheet we saw he had no face.
At dawn, I was turned inside out by thoughts of green and blue light. Cold
waves carried the spoils of sailors and travelers drowned in a distant sea.
You fight for life on the boats, and the sea swallows you before you land in
Lesbos, while I die in Sicily fleeing home. Don't believe Poseidon or
Ulysses's ship. Don't believe the letters and don't believe the words.
Nothing is left of Cadmus fleeing with his sister from Tyre in flames but
shards on a boat.

VOICE

I escape death on death's carriage
the sky casts me with ripped wings to flounder in my blood
and in
hers
I flounder
and all I gain is absence.

• • •

And now, in Damascus,
I have two images:
A fist smashes the door,
bleeding,
and an open forehead, knocking.
As if I were shrouded
in
what
I see
going into my fate.

VOICE

Is this the door to the house,
or are the shadow and I a door to the fantasy of the house?
The sun that was here
one day
on the down of youth
yesterday
and this door
a shadow standing
in the sun of my song.

VOICE

I return to open the door I shut
years ago,

I walk in a terrible emptiness
and the shadow that the house door gave as a gift to the sun
oscillates
in the shadow
and shatters
leaving my footprint soaked in the silence of my song.

VOICE

You want me in the clothes of a martyr
stretched out
in the water of your silence.
It's your dcomman
that I be
a flower
in the button hole of the shirt.

VOICE

Had I another fate
I'd go by no name
but the one you gave me
Oh Sham.
My little sister, you are
light
of the butterfly
in the winter of the world,
blood of history.

TABLET
II

In the constellation of Taurus I read my fortune,
I watched the bow that shot the arrow, as it passed the mysterious and hit
    the ankle of fate.
On the edge of the cliff

at the moment of the suicide's cry
I waited for the Daughters of Na'sh to appear.
I saw shooting stars
falling
and thought the mail was for me.

• • •

On a dark terrace of yesterday's surah,
I sat
ten nights
watching
but no caravan brought a companion
nor any bird brought back my message.

VOICE

Traveler in the dessert
my goal
is to get lost seeking the right path
and return from an eternity I imagined to a day on which no fruit perishes
or gold deteriorates.

VOICE

My blood doesn't want me alive
my blood escapes me
leaks out of my veins
shows me my trembling
My blood fills my hand
it spatters the rocks and the windows and the trees.
My blood
doesn't
want me
my love.

• • •

I'll tell my mother

I, the one afraid
of the depth of my blood:
Why did you give birth to me inside this book and leave me wavering in
    my fate
growing
inside its cradle?

VOICE

I stand in the Umayyad courtyard
and flagellate myself with chains
and keep flagellating until no part of my body is without a wound that
    cries for Hussein.
With the sword Zulfiqar[2] I bleed my skull.
Who am I?

• • •

In the Umayyad courtyard
finally
in the Umayyad courtyard
my body slices history in two
and allows the blade of the comedy to find the descendants of Muawiya
    and his son Yazid.

TABLET
III

Let's walk under the silent sky whose tongue is stone
walk over the years
walk and walk and become habituated
walk and send words from tongue to tongue.
Let's open the dictionary and greet the words
Let's open the papers and read on their pages what the poets wrote.
Let's walk barefoot on this silence, so no word is wounded.

• • •

Whose shirt is this, with the bloody collar
Whose jacket is this, on the peg
dripping blood
this footprint at the door
and this strange smell in the flower pots
the scream suspended in the sky of the house
Whose scream is it?

• • •

I'll walk with you and with myself
hear my footsteps on the corniche
one step in the shadow and one in the injured light
the shattered light, frayed at the edges
those who crossed yesterday are ghosts wandering in the burning light.

VOICE

In see-through nature I make you walk, in thorny nature
inscrutable and frightening
death advances gradually over laughter
happiness
is an earring glittering and lighting the esplanade
cry of March
his shirt and forearms.

TABLET
IV

I was waiting for a letter from another city
I was waiting for the sun and the moon in separate letters
but shadowy figures, dusty figures, veiled your day
and dispersed.
But now it is a dead night in a drowned night
and the sun and the moon are dying brothers.

• • •

If you were the boy of my gaunt hand, if you were my drowsy eyes
Who've seen and lowered their look
I'd be the silence of your repose on the grass
You'd be the puzzlement of an instant.

• • •

Your day is fate crying
destiny
and your life is water in the night.

VOICE

Leave the thorns on the crown
and the wood wounded
Leave the linen wet
and the twilight baffled by the blood of the one stretched out.
Your voice in a sea shell
a light emitted from the terrace of the past, the rose at night.
Leave me the pebbles of the beach
and push forward
so I can see the sea
wave after wave
the sail on the sea as the scream of the drowned.

TABLET
V

Next week
the week that came but didn't arrive
then arrived and found nowhere to sit
the week that
looks around
its shapeliness and demeanor triggering the craving of those waiting
I'll sit with you on the bench in the garden.
That's an old song.

• • •

I'll sit with you in the garden and you'll sit with me in my dream.

• • •

The garden I pulled from the book of things preserved sticks its tongue out
   at my little flower patch
forgotten in the corner of the picture.
My burnt little garden in burnt Gota of Damascus.
And Damascus is the terrace of Nimrod
a chasm in a body.

• • •

I'll write to you, Damascus, imprisoned behind the sun, a torn book in
   your shackled hands, your forehead split open by a rider's axe, blood
   screaming my name.
Blood that names me
and dies
My blood doesn't want me
Oh Damascus.

VOICE

Thank you
Thanks to this sea
to sad Izmir
to the virgin wave
that bore me from my mother's arms
to give me back the earth
for the earth, all earth, from this day, to be my grave.

• • •

Thank you,
Thanks to my gods who died on the ramparts
to Troy that burned
to the Greek ships
that didn't see me.

NOURI AL-JARRAH

. . .

Thanks to happy Europa
with the bracelets
that glittered for the teeth of slaves
her hands shackled by ideas
bleeding out
gold and silver.

. . .

Thanks to the people of beautiful Izmir
to the colorful fish and the quivering seaweed.
Thanks to the Asian gulfs that send me on biers on the waters
wrapped in my letter.

. . .

Thanks to the song of the singer
I have no face
for history to read its traces
or what Paul said to Peter
or what the exegete wrote in the margins of the massacre.

. . .

On the coast of the Aegean I saw my image clouded by others
I heard the gasping of the wave and the cry of the crab.
Thanks to the sea foam
to the flag
the jelly fish
and the squid.
Thanks to the sadness of the sand
on the shore under the sky of Troy
as the Greek ships sailed calmly on.

. . .

Thank you
Thanks to this silence
I heard the seaweed singing
to me

The bubbles snatching along with the laughter
at my old face.
Every face is a mask and every mask a lost soul.

TABLET
VI

And what if I had stayed that boy with the brown sandals and the yellow
    shirt and the sun in his words washed and pinned on a clothes-line.
What if I had lived sheltered with mothers filling the pitchers with
    mulberry juice and the corners of the house with whispers:
Let him sleep . . .
while the sisters listen and laugh
Was I going to live all that time, with an eye watching the world obliquely,
    the dark descending with axes.

• • •

How I renege in width and how I have fallen in height.
The television fills the house with images. My life is a silent reel.

• • •

Had I stayed, had I remained with myself, now, in the morning, in what
    night laid down in the house,
in the quick and the silent, the multiples and the units.
The heresy of the one who lay down in summer and dozed off and doesn't
    know how to get up, or how to return.
Because I am here, in this pit, my hand numb, as if the entire world were
    in winter and I its single inhabitant.

VOICE

I won a strange day on the sea
I won the light of an idea
a thin thread

to follow
in the dim light of your room
and my idea
but lost what the evening said.

• • •

I won a sun in the shade
and a maze
a step in your day, a flower in your sleep.

• • •

I won your voice startling
a mountain goat
on the roof of my day
wounded like a sun brought down by an arrow.

• • •

Between distractions
I saw a drop of blood
drip
from a planet
and the arrow in the river's heel.

VOICE

By your god, old stone,
By your god, oh moon, suspended from the depth of a pass
over the bay,
by God.
The ships aren't visible from here
the breeze said
the banners were folded in secret.
By your god, oh dusk, wrested away to distraction
in flames
gods slept on the images of their dying heroes, the sleep of herders dozing
    in the sun.

By God.
Who strewed the walls with burning linen
and toppled the talisman with the blood of the virgin?

TABLET
VII

Goodbye adorned carriage
goodbye to the almond wood, to the Damascene mother-of-pearl in the
    almond wood,
to the wind and what it withered in the Antioch summer
to the virgin hiding behind her charm.
Goodbye to Damascene purity, to Syrian bashfulness so brash in its
    embroidery
to the handkerchief
in the virgin's gasp.
Goodbye to the young peeking from high walls
and seeing fathers and brothers falling in tumult and shadow.
The gates close shut. Cawing vultures hover over the arches.

• • •

Goodbye to the blind man's stare into the scent of oleander, to the
    shadows,
to the mulberry tree in the burning dew
to the waving of the cripple at the gate of the souk
Here charm dies in its sleep and youth withers in the light of the spear.

VOICE

I say goodbye to the north. Burnt citadels, crops left to the beasts of the
    wilderness,
villages behind hills lefts to vagrants
the blood of livestock spilled along the coast
for the soldier to march
with his sword.

Pity Syria, lost like an anthem torn by a wind storm
pity her children in their nightly chat
pity the thirst of girls, the pain of voice
pity my anthem
with
no
end.

VOICE

I came down from a mountain in Damascus
I came down
in the sun of Jupiter
and in the joy of the children I saw the laughing ribbons of blood
the city had no god to describe the smile of the crescent.

• • •

I came down into the skin

of the screamer
I made the stone speak your feminine name.

• • •

The plants on the marble arch in the sun's cry
they too leaned down
and presented their offer to you.

• • •

The wish set the hour
and the traverser
pained the shade.

• • •

With hammer and chisel and a map of your back
I came down
Barada had no name, nor had illusion a lover.

• • •

And now, in the setting and darkening, in the slanting shadow, in the
    laughing, in the sun at the end of the day, in the water's scream, in the
    coquetry of youth, the pages bleed and the words leak out along with
    nothingness – take me by the hand and let the breeze tousle my hair
let me see
what's in the eyes
and let me ask
I'll be capable of nothing but this silence
gift from my heart to what's left of my step.

VOICE

And in another tablet, the fugitive said to the sea
leave me a handful of air inside a clock
a tower cracking in a beat
a strike of blind
luck
so I can be
on track every . . .
In what time has shed
and in what
never
was
neither in the north
nor in the south
nor in the true east, where the ibex's blood darts.
The shadows spattered eternity in bloody sheets.
There a woman seer said what the one with closed eyes said to the
   sleeping woman
and what was painted in the picture
without pain
or words.

VOICE

I came down yesterday from the mountain
Cain wasn't there
yet
nor the crow's wing
Abel, heedless, was looking at himself in the river's smile.

• • •

I came down the mountain, I came from the north,
the Euphrates was an idea
and so was the silt
and the traverser was, if only in the imagination of the listener, the idea
   of one sleeping in earth.

• • •

GREEK TABLET
(The Call of Sappho)
VIII

Dying Syrians, trembling on the shores. Syrians wandering across the
earth. Don't fill your pockets with dead earth. Leave that earth and don't
die. Die in metaphor not in reality. Let language bury you in its epithets.
Don't die and be buried in earth. The earth has no memory, just silence.
Set sail in all directions. Win the tumult of your souls. And after the
storm and the damage, rise in every language and every book and every
appointed time and every imagination and surge in every territory and
rise like the lightning in the trees.

London, summer 2015 – winter 2016

From the poet's collection *Qarib ila Lesbos*,
published by Dar Al-Mutawassit, Milan 2016

Notes:
1 The Daughters of Na'sh, Banat Na'sh, is the name given in Arabic to a group of seven stars in the
northern constellation known as Ursa Major (or, more commonly, al-Dubb al-Akbar, the Big
Bear). In ancient Arabian mythology, Canopus killed Na'sh, and his orphaned seven daughters
swore not to bury their father until they had taken their revenge on the killer, who fled to the
southern hemisphere. The four virgin daughters are still carrying their father's coffin, and the
three other sisters follow them – the first pregnant, the second carrying her infant, and the third
limping behind. (One of the English names of the group of seven stars is the Bear, but it is
commonly called The Plough or The Big Dipper.)

2 "The One with the Vertebrae", is the name of a sword believed to be one of the Prophet's swords,
given as a gift to Ali, the father of the martyred Hussein, whose death is marked every year by the
Shia in a ritual alluded to in the poem.

MONIR ALMAJID

Qamishlo

TRANSLATED BY JOHN PEATE

Qamishli has various names depending on which of its communities is speaking. My mother used to call it Qamishlouki, and sometimes Qamishlo. 'Al-Qamishli' is what Hamada the engraver has carved in fine *thuluth* Arabic script on the wall of the town hall. It's Qamishliya in other dialects.

The city itself is only about a hundred years old, yet there are conflicting stories about its origins. It is certain that Jews were the first to settle in the site, which is divided into two by the River Jaghjagh. Its development, however, is linked to the Kisla French military garrison near Al-Baden plateau, only metres away from the Turkish town of Nusaybin.

Back then, most districts were divided along community lines: Assyrians lived in the west, in Al-Wusta and Manouk; Al-Hammam and Al-Besheriya were mainly Syriac and Armenian (in all their different branches), as well as other Christian sects such as the Chaldeans and more Assyrians. And, of course, each community had their own church. The districts of Al-Jumruk and Qad-door Baig in the west were mostly Muslim: Arabs, Kurds, Turkmens, Muhal-lamiyas, Awmariyyas, and Mardaliyyas. There were the Yazidis, too, who are not Muslims but are Kurdish nationals, or at least speak Kurdish.

The Jewish quarter is in the centre of the city. It was named 'Palestine' after the June 1967 War defeat just to annoy them. There's a humble synagogue there that is built out of mud and straw yet serves for all the usual functions: a 'beit knesset' for meetings, a 'beit tefilah' for prayer, and a 'beth midrash' for study: they teach children Hebrew there.

I wasn't allowed to learn Kurdish myself since the Pan-Arab nationalists were trying to obliterate Kurdish national identity, especially under Gamal Abdel Nasser's rule, under the separatist regimes which followed, and the Ba'ath Party and neo-Ba'ath parties.

The Kurds are in the majority on the East and West sides of Long Street (or Main Street, as it was officially called) that connected the town of Amuda in the west with Al-Malikiya in the east. What is strange is that the dialect the Kurds speak on the west side is quite different from that spoken on the east, as if it were Qamishli itself that had separated them.

The Qaddoor Baig district derives its name from a wealthy family that used to own most of it, before self-styled socialist governments came along with their far-reaching nationalisation programmes to combat the feudal and bourgeois enemies of the people and the Muslim community. Or so they said. Naming of places followed an easily understood logic, evidently coming from the Assyrians and the Jews. So the Manouk district in the south was called after the Armenian owner of the flour mill there, and the district of Al-Jumruk in the east after its customs house, jumruk being the word for such a building.

Qamishli was always full of life, benefiting from the boom in the region's agriculture that consequently drew migrants in like a magnet from everywhere else in Syria. It was like a miniature version of the nations of historical record built by immigration, such as Canada, Australia, New Zealand, the United States, and countries in South America.

Qamishli had everything: parks, restaurants run by Armenians and Aleppines, a swimming pool for men, women and children to use any time of the day, and that, at night, turned into a kind of cabaret, with Damascene and Aleppine dancers shaking their fulsome hips and baring their bellies. The rich men of the city, with their ten-metre-long Chevrolets, lit their cigars with paper money, swelling with the hip-swaying vigour and sweet complexions of the ladies.

The city had its share of beggars, drunks, pimps, and whores too; it had its bars and taverns, its musicians and singers who were stars of many a raucous wedding. Each community has its own church, as I mentioned, and there are two mosques called – true to Qamishli logic – the Big Mosque and the Little Mosque. The Big Mosque faced Al-Arasa meat and vegetable market, only 500 metres from the brothel, on the same street. Our Aleppine neighbour, Abdurrahman, the mosque's muezzin, was fired because he used to visit the brothel regularly after climbing the lofty steps of the minaret to deliver the call to prayer in his loud, melodious voice. He was caught red-handed leaving the mud and straw brothel, perhaps after a tip-off from some envious person or other. He soon found another job singing Aleppine 'mawwals' and 'qaduds' at weddings, and became known as Rahmo from that point on. The Little Mosque faced Qaddoor Baig from Main Street.

There were two printing presses too, with some enterprising types publishing a magazine and a few fairly unimportant books.

There were two brothels in Qamishli in the 1950s: the one on the airport road was closed at the end of the decade for some reason that I'm not aware of; the second – the one I mentioned earlier – was on the edge of Al-Baden plains, a small strip of land separating it from the fruit and vegetable fields of the renowned Abou and a forest of white poplars that looked like pretty girls flocked around by sparrows that hopped around their branches, twittering with their familiar carefreeness. Mottled snakes and frogs would quickly disappear under fallen fruit and leaves. These were the sparrows that drew us into the forest, when we were children, in order to hunt them, though at the risk of being chased out ourselves by Uncle Abou, as we used to call him out of respect.

The Cultural Centre was a refuge from the summer holiday heat. Its ceiling fan used to circulate hot air while our fingers left little humid imprints on the books, magazines, and newspapers. Even so, the Centre was more merciful than our sweltering homes. The librarian was virtually illiterate, though he did know how to write his own name. Quite a contradiction, an illiterate librarian, perhaps the first in the history of humanity, but there you go, that's Qamishli for you: anything is possible there.

I myself am from Qaddoor Baig. I went to school there, knowing only a few words of Arabic. I grew the first hairs on my chin there. The locals were not only Kurds; there were Mardaliyyas there from the Turkish town of Mardin, and Muhallamiyas from the countryside around Mardin; there were people from Aleppo, Antakya, and one Syriac family that seemed to have got lost on the way to somewhere else, so settled in the neighbourhood; there were Circassians, Chechens, and folks from Deir Ezzor; there were Soviet petroleum engineers who had set up in Dr Al-Qanawati's hospital after he died suddenly; there were government workers; and there were both undercover and uniformed policemen who came from most of Syria's regions.

There was a solitary Christian cemetery in the north of Qaddoor Baig back then. The inscriptions on the tombstones were written in Arabic or Syriac, and sometimes there was a large cross over the grave, depending on how well off the family was. I was surprised to learn later on that the cemetery had initially been established for Jews, as the Hebrew inscriptions to be found there testify to. The sole Muslim cemetery was a mere half kilometre east of it, but it was not as well organized as its Christian counterpart, but rather carelessly and randomly arranged. We used to go to the Christian cemeteries when we were seven or eight for bread and dates which the families of the dead, as was the custom, used to give to mourners. We would chew on the delicious bread fresh out of the bakery as we followed the cortège to the centre of town along the old railway station road. If we got the chance, we would grab any young stragglers by the collar and make them recite the Islamic Shahada, or testimony of faith '*La ilaha illa Allah*', 'There is no god but God'. We would then let them scurry back to their families in panic.

There were always fights with the Christian kids in Al-Besheriya District. The older children were led by Wa'dou, one of the chief Qaddoor Baig ruffians at the time. They'd let us know the date and time of any battle, and we'd arm ourselves with sticks and stones, knives and sharp implements being completely banned. We would meet up, separated only by Main Street, and start throwing stones at one another before joining up for a ruckus in the middle of the street. I used to slip away unnoticed because, to be honest, I wasn't brave enough for fists, sticks, and stones. I was an emaciated, skinny little thing, a badly tied together bag of bones.

To the west was the River Jaghjagh, its muddy waters descending from the Taurus mountains flowing peacefully like one of the great rivers. Later, the Turks' building of a dam left its waters low in summer, its banks thick, bubbling mud, chock full of gas and effluent from Nusaybin and filled with wretched tadpoles gasping for a miracle in order to stay alive. The locals in Qaddoor Baig refused to pay heed to orders, and carried on strolling along its banks despite the dreadful smell, and the golden sand flying in from the desert of Iraq that stung their faces like needles.

The city was perishing cold in winter due to the north winds that would turn the air into ice and freeze your fingertips, making them feel brittle as biscuits. In summer, however, Qamishli was a hellish cauldron, its streets maddeningly hot. The temperature would get close to 50 Centigrade by around midday, and the powerful, scorching rays of the sun ruled over everything and blinded us all. At such times, the locals would seek shaded refuge from the dry heat. Those who wanted to show their wealth off by building houses out of concrete suffered even more, the idea of insulation never entering anyone's head back in those days. One of our neighbours who fell into the trap of building such a home was obliged to buy a refrigerator – unheard of back then – and huddle around its open door until they numbly dozed off. It was many years later before air conditioning came to Qamishli. By contrast, spring brought fresh air and pleasant temperatures, pushing us back outdoors and into the streets and surrounding fields. Autumn, on the other hand, would come in hesitantly, its lowering humidity portending change before it finally banished summer's horrors with its first rains that turned months of accumulated dust into a muddy soup with a silky texture.

In my teenage years I fell in love with a beautiful Syriac girl who had the blue eyes of a Swedish actress. The most I ever got from her was a smile on those summer evening umsiyat, as the people of Qamishli called the nightly comings and goings on Al-Qowatli Street that stretched from nearby Saba' Bahrat Square from the city centre southward cutting through Al-Wusta District and ending at Al-Uruba High School Square, where I went to school back then. We used to swig homemade wine from the house of my Jewish friend and classmate, Isaac, the taste of which I'll never forget.

We used to pay home visits to one another on holy days. My Syriac, Armenian, Assyrian friends would come en masse, greeting everyone with "*Kullu 'aamin wa antum bi-khayr*", "May all be well with you every year". That's what everyone would say before drinking a quick coffee with some chocolate or delicate green pistachio Turkish delight. Our much celebrated and very handsome teacher 'Isa was guest of honour there in my later years before I left for Damascus. He would always pontificate about matters he hadn't much clue about, even insisting once that Beethoven's Tenth was his best symphony. I used to follow the same rituals on my friends' holy days too, saying exactly the same things. The priests and bishops of the various churches, wearing their glorious vestments, would sit shoulder to shoulder in the mosques, on the same front bench with the senior officials and the imams, and the same would happen in the churches, depending on which of the numerous holy days it was. I never knew which Islamic school I belonged to and whenever they asked me I would rush to ask my mother, who was never sure herself. Were we Shafi'i or Hanbali? She just wasn't sure. To her, Muslims were just Sunnis, and that was that. I never knew a friend of mine was an Alawite until many years later, when Hafez al-Asad overthrew his comrades and took power. I would always know So-and-so was Syriac when I heard him speak to one of his family, and an Armenian by the nickname he went by, which always, without fail, ended in '-yan'.

It's true we used to chase after the Christian kids, but only for the fun and futile pursuits children are always after. It's also true that sometimes mixed marriages led to crimes. A Syriac, for example, would never let his daughter marry an Assyrian, more for class than religious reasons. The biggest crime was when a Christian girl ran off with a Muslim boy. I never once heard of a Muslim girl running off with a Christian boy. The story goes (though it's probably just an old joke) that a Syriac girl told her mother she had fallen in love with a young man. Joyfully the mother asked who he was, only for her daughter to reply that he was So-and-so the Assyrian. That made her mother ask loudly and harshly what was wrong with So-and-so the Kurdish neighbour's boy.

That, then, is the Qamishli I knew; I know nothing of today's Qamishli. All

I know is that its people don't visit each other any more on those religious occasions; its men of religion no longer sit on the front benches of churches and
mosques together. Kids don't brawl with one another and make others say the
Shahada for a joke. They don't throw stones at one another now; they fight
real battles with each other instead, using light and heavy weapons, district
against district, even family against family, where once there were bonds of
friendship and trust. The Jewish community took fright and left for various
parts of the globe many years ago. Qamishli has been showered with shells and
beset by booby-trapped cars. Strangers have gone there, arriving among my
friends and neighbours, to blow themselves up, wrapping their genitals in tin-
foil to preserve them for the virgins that await them in paradise. Some of those
who cultivate their beards have taken control of areas nearby, ritually slaugh-
tering people like sheep on holy days, kidnapping women and selling them at
slave markets, forcing schoolchildren to write their sums in a new way: "One
plus one, insha'allah, equals two."

I know I will die without seeing Qamishli again. I know I won't be buried
with the bones of my family, but no problem: I want to remember Qamishli
as it was for me and not as it is now. And if I get to live again, I would surely
make all the same mistakes and do all the same stupid and trivial things all over
again, but at least I would try to stop what has happened in Qamishli in the
last few years before it started. Has no man ever changed the course of history
while it's happening? The place of my birth has become an obscure and alien
place to me but truly I still long for it. To lighten the burden on myself of all
this I have begun to squeeze my experience of those wondrous days of
Qamishlo out of my brain onto the following pages.

EXCERPT FROM CHAPTER 1

For the last few months of 1951, Siberia sent a relentless, bitter, freezing
wind Qamishli's way. Qamishli wasn't the target, of course; it just happened to lie on its hellish trajectory (if hellish is the right word for
something bitterly cold). It stayed that way until the end of February 1952.

The Taurus Mountains overlook the valley that extends from the outskirts
of Mardin to Qamishli, passing through Nusaybin. Nusaybin overlaps with the
village of Al-Muhammaqiya a little to the north-east, with the much revered
Berlin–Baghdad railway from Turkey intersecting them. There, the minefield-
riddled border prevents smugglers from carrying out their illegal trade, with
an abundance of such devices also between lying Nusaybin and the village of

Al-Hilaliya in the south west. The smugglers, for their part, have found a bloody solution to these challenges: they send their mules ahead through the mine-fields to open up a route for them into Turkey. We'd often hear explosions in the night and find nothing left of the wretched beasts the next day but stinking flesh and entrails abuzz with flies delighting in their feast.

They used to hold mixed marriage wedding parties in between Nusaybin and Al-Hilaliya sometimes, since people often made marriages across the bor-der. Music would blare away and the guests — men and women, in line with the unwritten law — would clap their sweaty hands in a riot of dance over-topped in a cloud of dust. An international wedding, you might call it.

On particularly splendid spring days we'd take a stroll down by the waterfalls just close enough to wave to the Turkish border guards holding their rifles of some sort or other. We could hear distinctly the songs of Zeki Müren blaring out of Nusaybin's cafés. We would soon turn our attention, however, to trying to catch little fish by stealthily creeping up on them in the shallows, only for them most often to bolt like lightning into deeper waters.

In that 1951-52 Siberian winter, the Taurus mountains remained capped with thick, glistening snow which, unusually, even reached the plains sloping down towards Qamishli. The birds that migrated seasonally from Russia, worn out by their almost interminable journey, couldn't find any food in their resting places that year, their chirrups like those of baby crows with feathers dotted white. Colourful and dirt-coloured birds alike, heading for the houses of Qamishli, desperately sought out food, but ended up themselves as food on people's tables. They were either easy prey for primitive traps fashioned in kitchens or, if they didn't fall for that trick, for stray cats and dogs who would lie low in the thick snow then leap out to catch the enfeebled birds that sur-rendered themselves to their fate.

March finally arrived to put an end, at last, to that long drawn-out winter. The aluminium rays of the sun pierced through the heavy, leaden clouds, bring-ing a particular kind of warmth mixed with a smell that everyone recognised but couldn't quite find an exact name for. I will keep it simple and call it the spring smell. The snow melted into the tumultuous waters of the Jaghjagh. Qamishli's spring sun would always restore a moonlit kind of tan to our com-plexions.

The Jaghjagh wound its somewhat crooked way until it reached the electric-ity station that lay south of the orchards, Uncle Abou's woods, and the whore-house. There it split itself in two: a mill was built on one branch of it, encircled by a pit letting the water flow through the generator's hidden machinery and pipework. The other stream wound along for a few metres before pouring its waters into what is known as the French Basin. Young boys used to swim in the water, diving in to try and impress the girls walking by. When both branches of the river reach Main Street, about half a kilometre further on, they pass under two bridges, for which the people of Qamishli came up with equally ingenious names: the Small Bridge and the Big Bridge. North of the Small Bridge lies Al-Kamal Al-Jasmani Sports Club and, beyond that, a hotel in front of which the taxis that fill the town with their black smoke and diesel fumes line up. South of the Big Bridge is an arid square owned by the Hotel Al-Sharq that takes in guests from the neighbouring villages. The square is filled with dozens of guest beds in the summer, where the guests are attacked by three types of mosquito drawn to the area by the river's humidity and the scent of villagers' blood. Beyond the hotel lies the famous swimming pool with its sky blue painted walls, and, beyond that, mud-built houses along the river's eastern bank. That's where we used to live.

My father was an immigrant, like much of the Qamishli population. For many years after the Sykes-Picot Agreement was implemented he lived on the Syrian side, but came originally from the Lake Van region of Turkey. Once he became a teenager, he gathered together his basic necessities in a bag, and began his crazy quest for knowledge. He travelled through many cities, towns, and villages, a pupil to numerous sheikhs in many places. He memorised the Qur'an and absorbed the teachings of religion. Whatever hours of the day or

NEXT ISSUE two authors from Syria

Lina Hawyan Alhassan   Maha Becker

night remained, he would toil away doing any housework going. This was at the house of Sheikh Umar, my grandfather on my mother's side, in the Jazira Bouta area near the River Tigris, where Turkey, Syria, and Iraq meet. He took a fancy to the daughter of the house and asked his teacher for her hand in marriage. So, once his schooling was over, he gathered up his possessions once more and left, but this time accompanied by his wife as they embarked on their fascinating religious journey together. They wanted them to sign up at the Register Office on the Syrian side of the Sykes-Picot Line on the outskirts of the village of Biyandor. All my father knew of Arabic was how to recite the Qur'an, though he knew how to answer when they asked him his name: Abdallah. What nickname was he known by? That was more difficult. Nickname was a word he hadn't heard before. After a deal of sign language and noisemaking, he answered "Abed Almajid", his father's name, and so, though his real nickname was "Sheker", that's how we ended up with our name in Syria.

EXCERPT FROM CHAPTER 18

The makeover that the Marwan Street pavement and road surface underwent soon deteriorated. The tarmac cracked and crumbled, forming holes, some small, some large enough to break a donkey's ankle. The cement paving cracked and fell apart too. The local council did nothing to fix it, and the ordinary citizens did not care either, so dirt and mud soon prevailed once again.

A new generation of children grew up, pissing and shitting all over the place, torturing cats that people had mercilessly kicked out of the house, chasing off mad itinerants and chickens alike with their stones. And, late at night, packs of emaciated, ravenous stray dogs would roam around looking for food in the bins, and menace, by growl and bark, anyone out walking in the street.

The women followed the custom of moistening their hair following post-marital cohabitation, though maybe that didn't happen. The young girls who had been drawing pictures with chalk before would suddenly develop little breasts and bare their backs in the street. Hasaniko, a fan of the dancing in Indian films, had returned to good health and resumed his beloved career performing dances at weddings. His brother married a repentant prostitute who was loved by young and old in Qaddoor Baig. She had white skin, wore a white scarf, and looked like a saint in an Italian Renaissance painting.

We would still stroll along the banks of the Jaghjagh even when its waters were low. The women and children would eat tabbouleh and the men would swig araq, cigarettes still between their fingers, while carts selling lettuce wheeled their way among the picnickers. Once we saw a woman quarrelling with her husband, screaming at him that she couldn't bear her life any more before throwing herself into the river. She lay there covered in mud until the rest of her family hauled her up out of the ankle-deep water. Her husband remained sitting where he was the whole time simply shaking his head. That tale of a novel type of suicide bid was talked about by the people of Qaddoor Baig for years afterward.

Uncle Abou cut back his forest of poplars some time ago, cutting back on the area he cultivated due to the lack of river water. That gave us easy access to Al-Baden plain, which overlooked Qamishli and Nusaybin from the north. The lucky among us dug up a few coins there dating back to ancient times. Al-Baden was said to have seen a number of civilisations come and go, and the strange emergence of that hill on a vast plain was due only to an earthquake that had erupted and turned everything upside down.

People would hold their wedding parties there quite aware of any political changes taking place and of the presence of intelligence agents too, since they required a permit from the security services. The latest fad became microphones and amplifiers at such events, and the walls of the houses would reverberate with the dance music, meaning no sleep for anyone, young or old, who elected to stay at home. The drunken vocalist singing "Az Kevoké Lélé" – a famous dance song by an Iraqi Kurdish singer – and the ululations of the women would pervade the whole of Qaddoor Baig, and, to please the intelligence agents in our midst, the singer would give renditions of tunes by Farid El Atrache and Sabah Fakhri.

There was a string of gypsy encampments along the road eastward to the village of Al-Antariya. The women would spend the day knocking on doors begging for food, and the people of Qamishli were never so stingy as to not put a little something of their food into these women's bowls. People were always surprised by the strange mixture, and some would complain to their wives if they put too many different types of vegetable in their food that their food was like that of the gypsies.

At night, the men of Qamishli would race each other in their Japanese pickups to the gypsy camps, whose men would lay out mezze and glasses of Johnny Walker whisky, while any women present would put on lipstick and change into scandalously revealing dresses ready for a lewd night punctuated by whisky and sexy dancing, their husbands playing their tambours.

My brother bought a little Sharp transistor radio and listening to it became an obsession for me, especially in the evening. Voice of America was my favourite station, and from it I got to know Greek songs, Enrico Macias, Charles Aznavour, the Beatles, the Rolling Stones, and whatever the listeners had requested. I became a disciple of the programme's presenter (of Druze origin) Kemal or, as he called himself, 'Casey' Kasem.

I used to go and see French New Wave films at the Dimashq and Shahrazade cinemas without actually understanding anything about them. I adored Italian films, and got to know Soviet films for the first time there too. I took a quick look at a few Indian films, only to then avoid them for the rest of my life. In the Shahrazade, my immersion in the wonderful world of film reached a whole new level with "Il Vangelo Secondo Matteo" (The Gospel According to St. Matthew). Iskander Karat, Qamishli's cinema poster maker, wrote out the title of Pier Paolo Pasolini's famous film as: "Matt's Second Gospel."

One day a strange convoy of buses came to Qamishli and the Armenian families in the town gathered what little they had left of their possessions and disappeared in them. They migrated to Armenia, among them my friend, Hakob.

I was pale, skinny and cowardly, and would never join in with the fights among the young boys or the children, as I said before. Some days the pains in my left side immobilised me for hours at a time. It scared my mother and my eldest sister, and when the tests the doctors put me through revealed nothing, they made me lots of fruit juice to drink and more and more raw eggs to eat, something I did not relish.

The school study area began at Ayousha's house, the last home on the eastern end of the Old Station Road, and a few paces before the Christian cemetery. We used to hope we'd see Ayousha before we began reading in earnest, because that girl was never far from the minds of local boys a few years older than us. She was pale-skinned and beautiful, and a little full-figured, but we could breathe in the scent of her body that sent out invisible signals of temptation. We were a little young for her, so she never gave us those smouldering looks that went over our heads instead to the older boys.

Once, when I was on my early morning journey to study with my books under my arm, I saw something quite remarkable. A donkey laden with two large saddlebags of stuffed watermelons on its way to the town market happened to come across an unladen she-ass heading back to Al-Muhammaqiya. It seems she caught his eye because he stopped and turned his head towards her with quivering lips, unfazed by his owner's stick urging him to carry on. While he stood braying, his penis, which was huge out of all proportion to his frail, little body, shot up to attention as if a battery had been plugged into it. In a sudden acrobatic movement the donkey shook off his watermelon load, causing some to shatter and the rest to roll off in all directions. He ran a semicircular path towards the female, whom I feel sure he'd met before, slid himself on top of her, and jerked away spasmodically while she made strange grunting noises. The creatures' respective owners just stared at them, sensing there was nothing they could do about it. This all happened in an instant. Suddenly, Ayousha appeared at her door to see what all the commotion was about. A crowd gathered – men and women, boys and girls – to watch what was going on, all with different expressions on their faces. Ayousha was in her nightdress through which you could see her two nipples standing out like pebbles, quickly making her the new centre of attention. Everybody turned their heads towards her, leaving the two beasts to go at it, while Ayousha kept her eyes on the defiant donkey, and I could see on her face a smile of lascivious bemusement. As I recall, I dreamed of Ayousha many a night after that.

We also used to walk sometimes to the outskirts of Al-Muhammaqiya, and then turn eastward towards the railway station. At the station, we would sit in the shade of the train wagons, which smelled of grease, metal, and wood. Sometimes we'd sacrifice half a franc by putting it on one of the rails when a train came, half flattening it and wholly defacing it. If we got the chance when the train was taking a breather to regather its strength, we used to speak English to the Europeans sitting in the carriages on their way to Baghdad.

Preparing for my secondary school diploma, I joined the herds of students carrying books to the study area further along the road to Al-Muhammaqiya, swapping glances with the local girls at the same time, like kids have done since time immemorial. On sweltering days, before we could go off on our hikes, we used to bury our head in books, and waste a lot of time stopping for moments to reread a paragraph to ensure it was stored away in our stimulated brains for the big day. The big day that would once and for all lead us into the world of men. In the middle of the exam, and while we were fretting over answering the questions in the Arabic language section, they took away our papers and asked us to go home. The 1967 Six-Day War was at its most intense at the time.

MOHAMAD ALAAEDIN ABDUL MOULA

Seventeen Poems

TRANSLATED BY PAUL STARKEY

TWO DAYS AGO

Two days ago, perhaps two years, I took shape as a deserted moon in the
    mist of the oceans,
a well with broken shadows amid shifting sands,
I lost the smoke compass leading to the flame,
I remained like death altogether,
surprised by rain in the garb of absence,
I did not raise an umbrella or run away,

only begged it to tread gently with the rotten bones of the spirit and not to
   make of them food for its floods.

The rain still enjoys the temper of madness.

WHAT DO I LACK?

I make ready the cup, the crust of bread, the olive flower, the stone
   pistachios. I lack only my hands.
I make ready the ships, the shores, the travellers, even the farewell flags. I
   lack only the sea.
I make ready the bed, the dream, the explanation, the morning light. I lack
   only the woman.
I make ready the tombstone, the grave's dimensions, an extensive
   arrangement of cypresses, and a jug of water to water the plants after the
   burial. I lack only death.
So I begin, I lack only the ending.

THE ANATOMY OF LANGUAGE

Language enters the house of obedience
Creation leaves through the narrow window, fleeing into the blue.

Language enters a sea
Unknown fishes make a wedding for the sailor.

Language enters between your breasts
The tyrant feels danger.

Language goes out to the watery sidewalks drawn on roads above
The bats of the statues flee from their eyes.

Language goes out to the forest
All the love gazelles wander in the shadow of your dress drawn across the
   earth.

Language goes up to a roof, where your underclothes are drying in the sun
She is seized by lust as a memory quivers in her head.

Language mounts your bed
and with her go magical beings staggering among the cups of her magic.

Language does not sleep
She is not shaded nor does she cast a shadow
She does not kill
She does not cut off a poet's head
She does not burn the record of clay
or hide the clay tablet on which a lover has forgotten the smell of her breast
    rubbed with olive oil and the warmth of ginger
She closes no homeland, opens no prison camp.

Any language apart from that cannot be relied on . . .

METHINKS

1
Methinks I am a dried up moon
(Not like the moon the poets claim)
No light or pleasure in it
nothing but rocks
and two hollowed out crevices
friendless
sinking down, thin, with bones protruding
All those that claimed I am a lover's face
lied, then slept.

2
Methinks that for my sins I need the fire of the Magi
and two overflowing rivers of regret
and that all the temple chairs
are not enough for my confession
For who can undertake to forgive this great error?
Who persuade the heart in me
that the path of beauty is the straight one?

3
Methinks I am not myself
My ode has fallen from the wall of gold
Shepherds asleep and raiders everywhere
I still guard an ancient house
that has split under the thunder
I still pierce beneath my skin
that the flute may spread above my song
True, I deserted my parents
but I care not for Rome or Andalus
nor for the caravans from the entrance to Syria to the Negev
I have sold all the baggage of my heart
and preserved nothing but a piece of wood
which I shall light, that the newcomers may believe me,
believe that I am the scion of the Arabs

SLEEP NOW

Sleep now
Move a few missiles from the opening of the window
Wrap all your shadows in a little gentleness fleeing from the forest of the
    dead
There in the distance are the caravans of leaders borne on skulls
Yours are none of the abandoned bones on the road to the defenceless
    village
This East is tried by gods who shed blood with their lofty revelation

Sleep now and roam in our poetic state
Take from my veins a companion who will make meaning drunk with his
    songs
Do not hesitate to carry the cluster of languages
though concealed behind an impossible dawn

Sleep now, my beauty,
in the beautiful . . .

EMPTINESS

Emptiness: for you to sleep alone in your bed in the East, kept company by
    missiles that tune for you grey dreams
while I sleep alone beyond the oceans, having prepared for the spider his
    house in my bed.

Once I thought that my bed and yours were two wings . . .

GLISTENING RAIN

At night, in your name, the tame rain glistens
My land is light as a feather in your hands
and the trees that whisper near my window shine
as though your eyes were raining on me and them
a heaven of my language in your bed
From your bed your exquisite spirit records for me my song
more than a lover's bush at dawn will
Build a dream in your imagination or clasp your hands
in a trance of moonlit passion over an infatuated fire
The things around me tell you: you are like me, a fragrant flight
that no one can stop, so how should I want to tame the boundaries?

A WOMAN'S TERROR

How I am pained by a Syrian woman
Night and day the spectre of death spreads among her thoughts
She is eaten by the terror that crouches in her eyes
She walks in the cracked paths of a dream
sheltering in her hands what she can of the power of the spirit

A Syrian woman
frightened by the dream of freedom!

A PHOTO

Do you recall the photo in which you appear like a word sent down by
    God?
Yes, yes, the photo in which the rivers flow from your shoulders down the
    curve of your back?
The photo in which you smell of the perfume Tango?
The photo in which tears flow over your baby girl, which we made
    together?

Do you remember it?
Okay, I haven't taken this photo yet . . .

GOING ON

The sonnets will not stop so long as there is a moon
The pelicans will not stop their dance so long as there are lakes
Your breasts will not stop their upward stroll so long as there are
    mountains
My hands will not stop beckoning to you so long as planes take off and
    trains whistle
though I know that the earth will not stop receiving martyrs so long as
    there are tyrants great, small, and of all sizes.

CHANGE

Everything has changed, even the number of martyrs and the counter of
    dreams
the resting place of memory, the foothills of the sun

The knives' colours changed when they left their hobby of peeling
    vegetables
for the peeling of skulls

The children's voices changed, no longer caring for the voices of mothers lazily making breakfast as they gossip on the telephone

The smell of the graves changed after drowning in blood

The geography of the earth has changed
The houses' roofs have become the ground
Windows are broken seats for cats slaughtered by too much love
Cats that have lost their language: should they mew or howl?
Only the killer has not changed

COUPLETS

My hand is not cut off
but the air between our hands is rock

My foot is not lame
It is the dust trying to tame the graves

My eye is not put out
The earth is a workshop of corruption with chimneys of bones

My body is not a closed door
What should I do when the keys rattle on the neck of the wolf?

THE CEMETERY WATCHMAN

Every midnight the cemetery watchman listens
not knowing whether it is the moan of a dead man between two graves
or the moan of a dead man with no grave under the thorn tree.
Every night he goes to inspect his kingdom
and distribute portions of dreams to the dead
then returns to his wandering grave.
Last time, he noticed a hand stretched out to the gravestone from inside the
    grave
to erase the dead man's name, and write: Here lies Syria.

SYRIAN SNOW

1
Snow is the temporary grave of the world
and yet when it leaves it may bear dead men whose hearts are whiter
    than it

2
Snow in the Syrian night
is a tyrant whose whiteness will not hide the blackness in its heart

3
Snow is eloquence, which is not neutral
and is often spoken out of place

4
We squeeze the sculpted stones on the city gate
We feel the scorpions of the myth
Grandmother! The soothsayer said to us:
These scorpions protect our night from the snow's iniquity
Why did they pour down on us when we touched them like ice made of
    blood?

THE FALLEN MAN

In a single minute they agreed on how to kill him
In a single minute they agreed on the size of the winding sheet
In a single minute they agreed on the size of the place for his head in the
    grave
Not too wide, no grass in it, not even a match, or a piece of sky
In a single minute they filled in the earth
In a single minute they received condolences from his neighbours in the
    other graves
......
But till today they have still not agreed on how to inscribe his tombstone.

BEASTS

I do not find them here, I do not find them there.

The forest has bred its beasts
Trumpets of blood made better miracles of bones
How should burned bodies still be revealed to the morrow
when in the paths of the orchards blaze knives inscribed with a historical
    date?

I do not find them here, I do not find them there,
Sons of the morning spread between two beds of dew
I do not find the voice of the nightingale weary of silence
I do not find the sea's grandchildren ploughing pearls in their wives' dresses

I do not find . . .

I can almost see, even in the fates of men, the sperm of the beast.

DREAMS

I made a collection of dreams beside my bed
I cleansed them of the places that had aged
I carefully dressed them in delicate women's clothes
And forbade them even the sound of a war drum

In my sleep I saw only a smashed door knob at the entrance to our house
and the black dress of a woman carrying a silent god on her back
as she descended the staircase propelled by children whose bones rattled
    under their flesh.

Tomorrow night I will give the woman a white dress
and lower the god from her back
then break the staircase with a rock I have hidden for the black day.

منتدى العلاقات العربية والدولية

The Forum for Arab & International Relations

The forum for Arab and International Relations
is hosting a conference on

Translation and the Problematics of Cross-cultural Understanding

(3)

December 2016 12-13
Doha, Qatar

منتدى العلاقات العربية والدولية

The Forum for Arab & International Relations

يستضيف منتدى العلاقات العربية والدولية
مؤتمر

الترجمة وإشكالات المثاقفة
(٣)

١٣-١٢ كانون أول/ ديسمبر ٢٠١٦
الدوحة – قطر

الترجمة

وإشكالات المثاقفة

بحوث ومشاركات المؤتمر
الذي نظمه
منتدى العلاقات العربية والدولية
٢٧-٢٦ شباط/فبراير ٢٠١٤

إعداد وتقديم
مجاب الإمام
محمد عبد العزيز

CARL DE STYCKER, MICHIEL SCHARPÉ
AND PATRICK PEETERS

Dutch language literature from Flanders: open, dynamic, multifaceted

Dutch language literature from Flanders is part of a greater whole. Of course there is no such thing as the definitive Dutch literature. There is Dutch literature in the sense of literature written in Dutch, including the work of authors from the Netherlands, Flanders, Surinam and anyone else writing in Dutch. Dutch literature does not co-incide with one or more countries either. Flanders is part of Belgium, a trilingual country, where the French- and German-speaking communities each have their own literature, which makes up part of French and German literature respectively. Due to the recent influx of migrants and refugees there is also a growing host of authors based in Belgium writing in other languages, such as Arabic, Kurdish, Russian, etc. Consequently there is no such thing as Belgian literature.

Linguistic and national boundaries may not coincide, but geographical boundaries do play an important role. The Dutch language region is more or less divided by the expressions 'above the Moerdijk' and 'below the Moerdijk', the north and south of the linguistic region, which form separate circuits with their own literary infrastructure (journals, publishers) and ex-hibit a number of their own peculiarities in several areas of life, to the detri-ment of their communal language and shared literary history. Few authors operate in both systems. The most important contemporary novelists from the Netherlands are unknown to the general public in Flanders, and many Flemish writers have failed to achieve popularity in the north.

Despite the fact that this single language region apparently falls into two

Bruges: photo by Samuel Shimon

systems, people currently still speak of one language and consequently one literature, that of Dutch. On an institutional level there is a great deal of collaboration and exchange. Flemish authors generally publish with Dutch publishers, and Dutch writers are included in Flemish literary magazines. Magazines have a readership from both the Netherlands and Flanders, the entirety of Dutch literature is taught at university, prize juries are staffed by people from both countries and Dutch language literature is promoted and perceived abroad as literature written in Dutch. It is thus clear that we share a great deal, but in this contribution to *Banipal*'s guest literature we focus on Dutch language literature from Flanders.

World War II was a breaking point for literature as well as society in general. After the holocaust there came a generation of young people who wanted to settle the score with literature that focused on detail, small-scale happiness, navel-gazing. For Flanders the big three novelists are Louis Paul Boon, Hugo Claus and Ivo Michiels. All these writers can be said to have produced work which was taboo-breaking. Claus with his masterpieces on the collaboration *De verwondering* (Wonder) and *Het verdriet van België* (The Sorrow of Belgium), Boon with his socialist novels about the man in the street, Michiels with his literary experiment.

When it comes to contemporary prose there are, roughly speaking, three directions to be distinguished: autobiographical literature, the historical novel and stories dealing with contemporary social and political problems.

In the autobiographical genre we have Tom Lanoye (*Sprakeloos*, 2009, published in English as *Speechless*, World Editions, 2016) and Erwin Mortier (*Gestameld liedboek*, 2011, published in English as *Stammered Songbook*, Pushkin Press, 2015) who have written loving and moving books about their progenitresses. Peter Terrin's *Post Mortem* (2012, published in English as *Post Mortem*, MacLehose Press, 2015) deals with his daughter's brain haemorrhage, while also exploring the boundary between fact and fiction. Dimitri Verhulst achieved public success with his novel *De helaasheid der dingen* (2006, published in English as *The Misfortunates*, Portobello, 2012) about his youth in a marginalised family.

Besides these autobiographical works there are also many historical novels. One recent success is a story on the boundary between biography and history, *Oorlog en terpentijn* (2013, published in English as *War and Turpentine*, Harvill Secker, 2016) by Stefan Hertmans, a novel in the tradition of W.G. Sebald, in which the author uses his grandfather's diaries to reconstruct his adventures during World War I, while also revealing the great secret of the love of his life, and his great sorrow. World War I was also a subject for books by Stefan Brijs (*Post for Mrs. Bromley*, 2011) and Erwin Mortier (*Godenslaap*, 2009, published in English as *While the Gods Were Sleeping*, Pushkin Press, 2014). In *Godverdomse dagen op een godverdomse bol* (Shithouse Days on a Shithouse Planet, 2008) Dimitri Verhulst tells the entirety of world history in 200 pages, and in his *Grote Europese roman* (Great European Novel, 2007) Koen Peeters tells the story of 20th century Europe.

There are also novels which deal directly with social problems. In the disconcerting novel *Wij* (Us, 2009) Elvis Peeters writes about the sexual perversions of bored, nihilistic teenagers. Yves Petry explores love and the complex problems it brings with it: *De maagd Marino* (The Virgin Marino, 2010) is based on the true story of a cannibal who went in search of a partner in order literally to devour him, while *Liefde bij wijze van spreken* (Love, So To Speak, 2015) takes a love triangle as its subject. All of these books deal with social problems with the aim of offering insight. In that sense they are an extension of the post-war taboo-breaking novels with their emancipatory intentions.

The Dutch language novel clearly covers a spectrum, from profound introspection, via a panoramic view of a time period and Zeitgeist, to a surprising view of geopolitics. This outline of current literature is of course regularly challenged by new voices entering the scene. In *Drarrie in de nacht*

(Drarrie in the Night, 2014) Fikry El Azouzi describes the life of loitering youths in a small provincial city, thus fitting into the tradition of the socially critical novel, while also striking a new note by writing from the perspective of the migrant. In the family saga *Haar* (Hair, 2016) and the ink-black, mysterious *Val* (Fall, 2015) Kathleen Vereecken and Roderik Six respectively have written two very different books, each masterfully exploring the human spirit and human relationships, and both exceptionally evocative.

In contemporary poetry we can distinguish three trends, roughly speaking, which have developed since World War II. Firstly there is the continuation of the more or less classical tradition in which classical poetic subjects are handled in traditional forms. The greatest poet in this style is undoubtedly Leonard Nolens, but Miriam Van hee, Luuk Gruwez and Roland Jooris also continue to publish eminent work.

Secondly, there is more experimental poetry, influenced by postmodern philosophy and making use of typical postmodern tricks such as mixing of highbrow and lowbrow culture, intertextuality, dislocation and free association. There, too, different generations can already be distinguished. A postmodern trend was introduced by poets such as Stefan Hertmans, Peter Verhelst, Dirk van Bastelaere and Erik Spinoy, with younger heroes such as Paul Bogaert, Jan Lauwereyns and Els Moors as the post-postmodern generation. The poets we present in this magazine, Tom Van de Voorde and Bart Van der Straeten, are still finding their way at the beginning of their careers.

Finally in Flanders there is poetry with a strong oral basis, making full use of rhetorical tricks, with the aim of generating a changing outlook on the world. These poets mostly debuted on stage and have worked the tricks of good performance into their verses: they are largely anecdotal poems, with funny twists and moments of real surprise. Charlotte Van den Broeck, featured below, and Delphine Lecompte are the most important representatives of this genre. Maud Vanhauwaert and Andy Fierens even blur the boundary between poetry and cabaret. So in poetry, as in other genres, literature from Flanders is open, dynamic and multifaceted.

Translated by Anna Asbury

KATHLEEN VEREECKEN

HAIR

AN EXCERPT FROM THE NOVEL

TRANSLATED BY MICHELE HUTCHISON

It was 1976 and the scorching summer showed no mercy. The rain would be more than two months in coming. Parks and recreation areas with bathing ponds streamed full, day after day. Green grass and shiny cars existed only in the mind now. Water was precious and each drop had to be counted. Or, at least, that was the way Suzanne would remember it years later.

The holiday on the Costa Brava had been planned months in advance. Their father had decided to drive all the way down in one go. And so Suzanne and her two younger sisters were lifted from their beds one August day at four in the morning and crammed into the backseat of the bright blue Ford Tanus, next to the cooler box containing sandwiches and unfizzy squash in pyramid-shaped packs for the journey. As the oldest, Suzanne was allowed to sit next to the door – 'keep the lock pressed down!' Hanna was next to the cooler box so that she could nap on a pillow placed on top of it. And Catherine, as always, was the middle child. Calm and sensible, she looked through the windscreen with her parents, reading out the names of the villages and towns or drawing attention to potentially important road signs from time to time. And when Hanna woke up and said in a weepy voice that she was hungry, Catherine pointed out the bakery just opening its doors in the next village. The croissants were warm and flaky and smelled irresistible.

Once they had got past Lyon, Suzanne began to finding waving at the increasingly scarce fellow Belgians worthwhile. Most of them waved back with a reticent smile at the girl with the blonde ponytail. Waving turned into a game with a magic charge. If they saw five Belgian cars in the space of five minutes, she'd be top of the class at school. If there were more than two people in each of them, she was her father's favourite daughter, even though he didn't let it show. And if in each car at least one person waved back, it was absolutely certain at this point in time she'd go to heaven when she died. Within five minutes, she saw five Belgian cars in which there were at least two people. But in one of the cars all of the people stared grimly ahead. She felt disappointment stinging her face and her stomach too, a little. She wouldn't go to heaven. Until she realized that the damage was limited. She'd been clever enough to add 'at this point in time' to her magical thought. Reassured, she rested her forehead against the window and smiled: her life stretched out endlessly before her. She had all the opportunities in the world to earn her place in heaven and she was completely confident she would manage it.

By the time they saw the Pyrenees looming in the distance, Hanna was vomiting into a plastic bag which Catherine was doing her best to help her hold. A blob of vomit had ended up amongst the comic books; specifically, right on Tintin's face.

'I said you shouldn't read in the car,' Catherine said with gentle reproach as Hanna's gagging announced the arrival of a new load.

Several miles before the Spanish border, the *route nationale* became congested. The multi-coloured ribbon of cars shunted along further, bumper to bumper. Suzanne felt the puddle of sweat under her bare thighs spreading over the black leatherette of the backseat. Catherine's hot arm which had almost felt like a part of her own body at first was now driving her so crazy that the urge to scream or to hit Catherine became almost irresistible.

'Are you sure you can't move over a bit?' she asked with restraint,

photo (c) Eugene Hertoghe

heaven in her thoughts, but her annoyance burned so brightly she jutted her jaw out as she spoke. Catherine's calm 'no' was justified, which made her even angrier. Hanna whimpered. It was hot. She was tired. She was hungry but mainly thirsty. When Suzanne finally tackled the litany of complaints head on by saying that she really, desperately needed the loo – anything to escape the suffocating heat and the oppressive physicality of the backseat – her dad slammed on the brakes, provoking a tense concert of toots behind them, after which he gave Suzanne a slap on the arm which had been meant for her cheek. She sobbed because of the unfairness of it. But she knew he didn't mean it like that. She was his favourite.

Hotel Solimar was on the seafront and resembled a Mexican *hacienda*, the kind you saw in *Zorro*. The shadowy courtyard was lined with concrete planters that were filled with little olive trees and oleanders. Young mulberry trees with espaliered branches were everywhere, doing their best to make the heat in the courtyard bearable. Spots of sunlight danced across the terracotta tiles and the faces and arms of the people dotted about on metal chairs with orange cushions, sipping from large glasses of sangria. Orange, Suzanne's favourite colour. If heaven was in Spain it would have looked like this.

Eduardo, the hotel owner, barely showed his face. From time to time, his colossal body shuffled through the lobby or across the patio on his way from nothing to nowhere and back. Ana, his equally bulky wife tended to shut herself away in a dusty, windowless, little office where she could avoid being troubled by hotel guests and the sun. It was Concepción, her childless younger sister, who manned the hotel reception. In the darkest corner of the lobby, far from fresh air and sunlight, a television set was turned on day and night, even when there was nothing more than the test card to be seen. During those moments, Concepción was reasonably approachable but when her favourite *telenovela* was being aired, most of them made in South America, she'd reach for the keys with reluctance.

And then there were Eduardo and Ana's children: Eduardo and Ana. The first was a shy eleven year-old boy who barely raised his head when addressed by a stranger. Awkward and nervous and, despite the constant rotation of similarly-aged children in the hotel, always alone. His sister was also closed off but in an almost otherworldly manner. Usually she stared into the distance with a childish expression of amazement that she was rather too old for at thirteen.

Why the Garcias, grocers for many generations, had decided to open a hotel seven years earlier remained a mystery. Was it because Spanish coastal tourism was taking off and their greengrocers business couldn't compete with the encroaching supermarket chains? Or had someone advised them to invest in property? And speaking of investments: where did simple folk like that get so much money from? The hotel guests speculated at length, a pattern that would repeat itself year after year without anyone becoming the wiser. But there was one thing that everyone agreed upon: the family didn't have a scrap of talent for it. Luckily, they had managed to attract diligent and even charming personnel. The maids were helpful to the point of it being embarrassing and the friendly bartender looked like David Cassidy. Suzanne always hoped he'd smile at her. When she walked past him with her sisters she'd invariably raise her voice to try attract his attention. And she'd laugh just a little too loudly, until he looked and smiled. But to be honest, he smiled at everyone.

The family moved into two adjoining apartments. Catherine and Hanna shared a double room. Suzanne got her own room with a view of the overgrown garden. She found a pile of well-thumbed romance novels in the wardrobe, left behind by a previous guest. There were strong-looking men on the covers, catching swooning women in their arms. Their titles promised her a world that was both terrifying and irresistible alike. *A Perfect Dream. Indestructible Love. Battle for the Heart. Bound by Desire. Memories of a Night. Summer Fire.* The bottom book had a flame red cover and the title *Who is Seducing Who?* At the top, big yellow letters proclaimed that the book was 'sexy'. Sexy. The word was itchy. When Catherine came in unexpectedly, Suzanne jumped out of her skin. Her sense of shame was worsened by the way her two-year younger sister looked at the pile with calm, grey seriousness. Astrid Lindgren was her limit, of course.

The beach was close by in the windy corner of the bay. Parasols had to be planted firmly into the sand or they would blow away almost immediately. Despite the wind, it was so hot you had to wear flip-flops to walk on the sand, otherwise you'd burn the soles of your feet. But even though the wind lessened the heat, Suzanne hated it. Not because of the sand that blew into her eyes, not because of her hair which was thrown in circles until it knotted. Simply the wind itself, which made her angry in a way she didn't understand. She observed the way her mother was reaching back with her arms, her head slightly raised, her eyes closed in pleasure as the thin tunic flapped around her body with brief, angry tugs.

'Lovely, isn't it?' her father said, as he tried unsuccessfully to smooth back his hair. Her mother nodded and they kissed each other gently on the mouth.

Towels had to be dug in at the corners or they'd blow away, bags containing bottles of suntan lotion and water were used as extra weights. But only that of her mother, who had settled down with a book – something by Simone de Beauvoir but later Suzanne could no longer remember the title – stayed more or less in place. With her smooth brown legs, large round sunglasses and her long dark hair bound by a turquoise scarf – or had it been purple? – she resembled a film star.

She should have spent longer looking at her mother. She should have paid more attention.

Hanna took off her t-shirt and ran towards the sea in her bikini bottoms, their father running after her. Catherine, too, was wearing nothing but bikini bottoms. She lay on her stomach on a wet patch of sand where the heat was bearable and stared tensely at nothing, or in any case at something miniscule in size. She carefully turned the sand with a stick, stabbed at something invisible and kept staring at it until she apparently had had enough and followed her father and little sister into the sea. Suzanne was wearing a bikini top for the first time, with a mixture of pride and shame. She was the only one in the family, her mother swore by a monokini and, with due kindness, laughed at Suzanne's prudishness. The swelling of her nipples was now too pronounced, Suzanne thought, and before she'd show her immature breasts to the outside world, she had to get used to them herself.

She began to walk to the waterline, slaloming between men with kites and children running after balls, sunbathers marinated in oil and shadowed readers. Her father had swum fifty metres out to sea with Hanna clutching his neck. The only part of Catherine visible was her shoulders and a snorkel, as would be the case for the rest of the holiday. Suzanne went to stand in the sea. A remarkably calm sea, despite the wind. No waves worthy of the name, just a stretch of water that quivered without breaking. She looked at the green paleness of her feet in the water, felt the pebbles under the thin soles of her flip-flops. She smelled the salt and the algae, heard the voices of people far away in the sea since that was where the wind was coming from. Walk further, deeper. And the deeper she went, the less she felt the wind. She let herself sink under water, long before the ground had disappeared beneath her feet. The sea was warmer than she'd expected, the water was soft. An unexpected consolation for a hitherto unsuspected sorrow. She swam and cried, salt in salt.

Friday night was disco night in Hotel Solimar. With a live performance by El Tío Paco – Suzanne's parents jokingly redubbed him El Tío Loca, a singer of around fifty with pitch black, lacquered hair, dressed in a white suit with sequins. Tirelessly and wholeheartedly, he sang his own version of new and not so new hits. While her parents preferred to soak up the gentle evening air and the muted sounds on the terrace, Suzanne and her sisters jigged around on the dancefloor. Hanna was boisterous and jolly, Catherine reserved, with a shy smile, and Suzanne composed, always conscious of the eyes of other people. 'That's the way, u-huh u-huh, I like it, u-huh u-huh,' they sang along at the top of their voices. When 'Dansez maintenant' started playing, the dancing became a little more embarrassing. And when the entire dancefloor went wild to 'Una Paloma blanca' Suzanne stopped joining in completely.

'C'mon Suzanne!' Hanna shrieked as she tried to drag her back onto the dance floor.

Suzanne shook her head and collapsed into a chair. She looked at the boss, Ana, who was dancing seriously with another woman, their bosoms pressed firmly against each other, swaying sisterly to the same cadence; at Paco who beamed as he sang; at the handsome barman, who smiled at a girl with long brown hair, dolled-up for the night with plum-coloured lips. She looked at her parents on the terrace, who had each other and were visibly happy with that. Her insides filled with emptiness, as though she did not belong here at all. As though she belonged nowhere, like in a nightmare. To unbelong, she thought, wondering if that verb even existed. But there was no other way to describe it. She returned to the apartment on her own, via the garden. It smelled fusty and strange there. Unbelonging. She turned on the beside lamp in the room she unbelonged in. The books still lay on the bed. At the top, *Memories of a Night*. Books that fell open, her mother had sometimes talked about that. She loved second hand books, she claimed, because they guided you to the previous owner's favourite passages. Suzanne set the book on its spine and it fell open instantly at page 99.

She read.

'I'm going crazy with desire for you,' he murmured, pulling her onto the bed in a fluid movement and rolling on top of her.
'Nicolas! Let go! Let me go, Nico!'
Her cries fell on deaf ears. He buried his face between her breasts and kissed her skin here, there and everywhere, until she, too, was swept along by his passion. She stroked his shoulders and ran her hands across the smooth skin of his back. He moaned and she felt him pressing his body even closer to hers, as he passionately found her mouth in a kiss that would leave her panting for breath.

'Suzanne? Are you there?'

Suzanne slammed the book shut and threw it quickly under the bed, along with the rest.

'Yes, Mum,' she said, as she came out of the bedroom to meet her mother.

'Are you all right? You disappeared all of a sudden.'

'I wasn't really enjoying it.'

Her mother smiled. 'No, I understand.' She stroked Suzanne's hair. 'You stay here if you feel like it.'

Suzanne nodded and gave her mother a crooked smile. When she was on her own again, she got the novel out from under the bed and carried on reading, as she began to feel less like an unbelonger. But how she did feel was difficult to describe. It was hot and extremely hot. In particular between her legs. And it filled her so much that she didn't seem to have space for anything else in her head. She thought only about skin and breasts, and passionate kisses and going crazy with desire.

Three weeks in Spain stretched out ahead of her. Three weeks that had seemed endless at first. But to her surprise, Suzanne began to feel like she belonged in Hotel Solimar. She felt at home on the beach and, yes, even in the wind. She swam and read, and effortlessly switched between comic book and romance novel, her mood changing accordingly. The heat between her legs became familiar. Sometimes it wasn't there, but from time to time it would suddenly materialize: when she was lying on the beach and the sun made her body glow, when she looked at the almost naked beachgoers around her, when she thought about David Cassidy from the bar. And sometimes for no reason. She even began to feel good amongst the hotel guests and the Garcia family with whom she had nothing in common. But habituation and familiarity worked their magic in an inconceivable fashion: the feeling of unbelonging ebbed away until she could hardly imagine that it had been there.

On the way back to Belgium, the car broke down and they had to stop. Her mother got out and walked back to the petrol station they'd just passed to get help. But before she had got there, a Spanish lorry mowed her down on the hard shoulder.

It was somewhere between Toulouse and Montauban.

About Kathleen Vereecken's novel *Hair*

On their way home from a holiday on the Costa Brava, Suzanne, Catherine and Hanna watch as their mother is mowed down by a lorry on the shoulder of a French motorway. From now on, father Ivo will do his best to raise their three daughters, but without great success. The three girls have difficulty establishing meaningful human contact.

In *Hair* the three sisters reminisce and take stock of their lives. What is left of their passionate childhood dreams and their youthful desires? How have the years of tension between sisterly affection and sibling rivalry coloured their view of one another, and of the world? And why does shame stick to each of them, like a second skin? Their father, meanwhile, is on his deathbed. His life takes place only in his mind. Ivo has let go of his shame, and with it his guilty conscience. He reflects on his daughters, on his wife and her untimely death, and on the secret that torments him.

The novel deals with the major issues surrounding love and betrayal and asks questions, such as: why are women so fond of ritualistically ushering out their youth? And why do they cut their hair short?

BART VAN DER STRAETEN

Four poems

TRANSLATED BY ASTRID ALBEN

NINE INFINITIVES

to have

do you have the discipline of carrion?
do you enjoy the smell of rotting fruit?

there's the child that screams for joy
it's the final chord of something

to come

come when it is time to harvest
when the world is in hiding
when life turns round

and the sky too swings round

dust to dust
ashes to ashes

back turned to the sun
back backed
to the flat, flat horizon

to turn

at their wits end and battled out
the words turn round
they have eyes.
they are watching me.

at their wits end and battled out
the words undress
they bare their teeth

the words are rapacious
the words are sick
they want to be healed

at their wits end and battled out
the words wore me down

at times you have to give each other the slip
a word is a bed like another

to reason

don't believe in load-bearing beams
too many things can fall

you will need your wits about you
from the town to the house
the distance is immeasurable

sometimes you step out, without purpose
for no apparent rhyme or reason, sometimes

to give way

don't value pleasure.

life's groundwork is simple.
you have to see it with your own eyes

we had nothing to declare
not even hope, which wouldn't give way.

we packed up early. is that
the groundwork for an explanation?

to sharpen

you would have been
non-recyclable
a eulogy for the funeral
an alarm clock that goes off

fodder for the vultures
fodder for the earth
a knife to sharpen

the smelting of letters
the processing of fat
larynx larder

to reveal

sometimes an answer will reveal itself
as fully inhabitable

you build

a literal house

you skim
the surfaces

enterable rooms
and tenuous connections.

in this sense wisdom
is also a shelter

your individual body
the property of the other

death is a city
changed in our sleep

to disturb

is it the chill in the air that disturbs
the damp driven up from the chimney
a veil covering your eyes
go, stoke up the blocks
sometimes we are
petrified

to try

don't be afraid

it is something that passes
in stages

there are those who keep trying

eventually
this too will pass

FOUR ISLANDS

1
like the quarry
of sensory waste

weighs in me
in me weighs
constantly

the bowline, bowing
to the subsequent,
emptier sea

2
from the cochlea
crows nest

forefather, forward
forwards father
ease off

the course, the wind
blowing behind
the wind

3
from the echoing well
head

breaks off the echo
breaks loose the echo
inward

looking, looming

sound
of the sea

4
words,
don't take

my place
from me
leave me

to fight
with you
fight against you

THREE WARS

1
how
now here

to extend
this existence

escape route
warrior heart

2
there are facts
thoughts
and deeds

combatable landscapes

without which
it's not

3
the reasons
behind enemy lines

envisaging

a lust for power
the rageing
the rage

system error

THREE SLOPES

1
you have to
overhaul everything

till it begins
to tilt

and then slowly

careens again

2

there is nothing
inside the volcano

that doesn't belong
to the volcano

or to the heat
that springs from it

3

chest puffed up
chin pushed forward

go to stand
at the tip of the seesaw

and jump
imbalance

From poet's debut collection
Onbalans (Imbalance),
Uitgeverij Vrijdag n.v,
Antwerp, Belgium

RODERIK SIX

Fall

AN EXCERPT FROM THE NOVEL,
TRANSLATED BY BRIAN DOYLE

It was still dark when I left Montreal; there was barely any traffic on Continental Avenue and I crossed Picard Bridge without a hitch, and as I left the city behind me, the dawn unfolded before my eyes, fresh and pink, and it was as if I was waking in unison with the earth, shaking the darkness from my back as it did.

I drove with the window open, determined to burn my left elbow.

First three hundred kilometres to Charlesville where I stopped for a steak, then five hundred to Capitol, slowly branching southward where the population thins; short distances, from gas station to gas station – the smell of coffee, stale toilet tablets and exhaust fumes, the corpse of a racoon on the roadside – through small, nameless settlements, no more than a few houses rubbing against each other, places where I slowed down, even turned the radio low, caressed the gas pedal with my toes, stealthily, so as not to wake anyone.

Somewhere in between I met a girl, Charlene by name, but she didn't interest me. We sat outside at a picnic bench and drank coffee together as we stared at the ten-tonners trundling past. She fidgeted incessantly with the loose threads on her frayed jeans and I bought her a hamburger. She looked as if she could use it. She had been beautiful once, and could be again with a bit of luck, albeit never quite the same as before: wear and tear had sunk its teeth in too deeply, and in a flash I saw her in front of me, many years later, smoking at the kitchen table, menthol cigarettes she stubbed out halfway in a metal ashtray, tea slowly getting cold, in a neatly maintained but otherwise unoccupied house.

'I'm Charlene.'

That was all she said, and she pronounced the words in such a way

photo (c) Studio Edelweiss

that she seemed to need convincing of her own name, as if she barely believed it herself.

She clearly wanted a lift, to anywhere as long as it was away from where she was, but I was already on my feet, intent on calling it a day, and as I walked toward my car and the dust swirled around my feet, I looked back half-heartedly one more time and waved – from a distance it must have looked like a gesture of dismissal, and maybe that's what it was: brushing off a vague possibility, a future we would never explore.

Late in the afternoon I took the last and only exit marked Fall. The country road was appropriately named Fall Road and consisted of two lanes, one there and one back, neatly separated by a white line, a long straight white line.

The evening sun smouldered in my rear-view mirror, and as each mile passed I drew closer to my ever lengthening shadow.

I passed an old billboard. A faded fragment of text, flakes of colour-less paint – a lost dream.

Only trees after that. Forest.

It was getting dark.

A talk show on the radio babbled on incomprehensibly. The volume wasn't loud enough to tell the voices apart, but it was statement enough that somewhere in a small studio people were messing with microphones and opinions. Some whispers in the dark, that's all I needed, that's all we are.

There was no oncoming traffic. It made me listless and impatient all at once. I missed the sudden appearance of headlights, those silver pinpricks that make you sit up straight, grab the wheel more firmly, consult all the pointers on the digital clock, briefly run your eye over the bag on the passenger seat – you're all set – and then it comes, and faster than you expect: the flash and the roar and the metal, that little air bump in the side, the tension in your jaws, eyes fixed on the road, your eyes at one with the red dots disappearing in your rear-view mirror, and then it's over and calm all of a sudden, the tarmac's your own again, stretched out in front of you like a black carpet, and you race ahead, alert, into the night.

Nor the reverse. The sluggish escort, the white light that crawls through the car, pasting shadowy fingers on the dashboard; the rub-ber band that hangs between you, stretching and shrinking but never snapping – the skin creeps in the back of your neck, you feel ex-posed, observed, uneasy, and you vacillate, hesitation cramps your calf – speed up, or slow down – but there's no solution, and there's a limit to the number of gnawing miles of this you can endure.

No, neither.

I was the only driver on this long, straight road. Mile after mile.

I became aware of my breathing. The weight of my legs. Felt the mass beneath me swell as if I was driving up a mountain.

I had closed the window. A steely cold had invaded my biceps and no amount of rubbing could shift it. As if something foreign had infected me, flourished in my flesh, and was waiting for the chance to stiffen my entire body.

My eyes had been struggling with the dark for quite some time.

The sunlight had chilled to a vague metallic sheen.

The white line: once a reliable guide that disappeared into the horizon, had now been pared to a hazy stump. And I might have been dreaming that too. Driving blind, staring ardently at some obscure smudge on my retina.

There was no avoiding it. I had to crank up the headlamps to full beam.

An old aversion. Light makes darkness visible. The nights you head down to the basement with a flashlight to check the fuses during a power outage. The thin cone of light that exposes mostly what you don't see: heaps of black, above and below you, an immense, breathing mass menaced by a miserly shaft of light. Like walking into an inferno armed with a water pistol.

The trees jumped into view at a single click.

All those trunks, those grayish forms, fashioned from faded marble – a petrified army standing in line.

As if holding still.

I remembered a playground game. Someone turned his back to the rest and recited a rhyme. As he spoke everyone was free to move, forward, in the hope they could pass the wizard by. When the words stopped everyone froze. The wizard looked back, peered around. If someone was still moving, lost their balance, moved a foot, blinked – they were out.

You could feel the silence at that moment, its weight. The suspense. The hesitation. The tension like a question mark in your muscles.

You liked being the wizard, but never said. Until you turned around again and felt everything shudder behind you. And closing in.

They were precariously close to the road, with greedy roots reaching out to the asphalt. As if their silvered stems were holding their breath.

Their crowns formed a roof over the concrete. Seen from above:

a thin glimmering scar between a billion green scales. From below:
a tunnel. Every buttressing stem the rib of a vaulting arch.

I automatically slowed down, leaning over the steering wheel to
look up with my mouth hanging open. The shadow of branches:
freakish, black thunderbolts on the glass.

Awe – that was the word. What you feel in cathedrals.

Nothing but static on the radio. The needle flickered, but couldn't
hold onto the signal. I couldn't bring myself to turn it off. I read once
that static crackle is residue noise, what remains from the big bang.
A foundational tone that sounds the same wherever you are in the
universe. The echo of a door that was once slammed shut, in the beginning.

I forced my foot to press the gas pedal.

Like an accelerating carrousel: one trunk after the other. None exactly the same as the one before, yet little by little a single ribbed
whole.

Black scratches on the glass.

Surges of current through the needle.

A swell of static.

The smell of wet leaves that forced its way inside via the air con
ditioning, pregnant with wood and green.

And then, a star.

I blinked. My chin anchored on the steering wheel to stabilise my
gaze. To the right, in the distance, between the foliage, unmistakable:
a star.

I slowed down again, afraid I would miss it, afraid I would drive
past. I briefly lost sight of it, but then it reappeared: a five pointed
star, white on a dark background. There, that's where I had to be.

A vague fear gnawed in the background. The fear of ending up like
the three wise men who chased a magnificent unreachable comet
towering high above them, only to have to settle for a baby in a stable.

You can always trust fear. And it's generally worse than you ever
dared surmise; most of the time you're not afraid enough. You always
brush it off a tad too lightly. It's nothing, just the wind, a nocturnal
breeze billowing through the curtains and caressing the hairs on your
neck. It's nothing, creaking timbers, a dry twig cracking in an abandoned forest, a rustle in the bushes, the shrill scratch of a black bird.
It's nothing, a shadow glides over the TV screen and you don't dare
look behind you. The fleshy sound of something slumping in the

fridge. It's nothing. The tickle of a spider's leg on a nipple, the flicker of a scalpel – it's nothing, nothing at all.

It was a sign.

Two metal poles and a board, half overgrown, with only a star poking out. A stupid symbol, a sign on a board. Not a comet in the heavens, or a guide, or a way out – not even a dry-nursed baby in a manger.

I exhaled some irritated air through my tightly pressed lips. It didn't help. My hands itched and the car suddenly seemed to have shrunk, all its glass, metal and fake leather just that bit too close. I turned the ignition key, testily, as if I wanted to pinch something really hard. The engine stopped with a sigh, or better said a relieved shudder. I immediately regretted it. I'd seen cars refuse to do their duty in too many films; too many bank robberies with sputtering getaway cars, too many flooded carburettors as the maniac with the chainsaw gets closer and closer. Too much flickering celluloid with reality glimmering through. But too late, always too late.

I threw open the door in agitation. A rush of cool evening air against my cheek. I stepped out of the car too quickly, too rashly. I was immediately less. Diluted.

A low mist hovered in the headlight beams. It wriggled from between the trees, crossed the road languid and unruffled, and disappeared between the trunks on the other side. I also felt misty, as if the slightest breeze could fray me apart. Breath surrounded me – the cold vapour of the forest. Its grandeur menaced me, me, here on this narrow strip of asphalt, alone, on a godforsaken evening.

I embraced my arms, to hold myself together, and walked toward the sign, trailing my shredded existence behind me.

I clung to details.

A seed tuft hovering just above the mist, a featherweight orb with white tentacles of the finest hair playfully exploring the world. A leaf let loose from its branch, flurrying past in a fluttering spiral.

I wished I was an ant, something puny, something more fitting to my size. Something too small to be scared.

I focused my eyes on the ground, no more than a yard or so in front of my feet. The sign had to be close. Yet it still kept me waiting; time transformed into a spider's web, the rarefied remains of a web, deep in the winter.

Then I suddenly bumped into the poles. They were hard and tangible, of lifeless metal. A neighbouring tree held the board in its grip: a hand of branches clasped the colossal sign as if it was about to rip it from the ground. The star glistened between the gnarled fingers.

I examined the claws of wood, my arms still wrapped around my chest – the tips of my fingers resting in the hollows between my ribs. I shivered involuntarily; to be able to see the rest of the sign I had to touch the branches, break them like fingers during an interrogation. Right away, even before the first crack, I felt a dry sound just below my jaw, like gravel in my throat, and I forced a yawn to swallow the hardened lumps. The cold met my teeth.

How was I going to reach it? The lower part of the sign was already at eye level and there was nothing in my car I could use as a step. And even if I could get close enough, I wasn't in the mood to blunt my scalpel on it. I briefly considered just leaving it be: dropping my arms, turning around, getting into the car and following that damned road to the end. What did I care about the sign and its secret?

Something in me seeped out. At once I was more stable, better defined – my body resisted once again and I felt my surroundings collide with me anew instead of flowing through me. I noticed things; the vicinity and its sounds.

For the first time since I got out of the car, years back, I heard the presence of silence: the ticking of the engine cooling under the hood, the gentle rustle of the crowns like the calm heartbeat of a sleeping monster, the timid hum of an insect skimming past, perhaps even the angular flapping of a bat in pursuit. The folding of moist moss under my soles.

And the singing.

Once, in a distant summer, I had heard the same under the transmission towers. Thin singing, as if millions of human voices pressed together were whooshing through the electricity cables high above me, racing toward their destination, the other side of the line. Every few meters, huge balls had been threaded like beads over the cables, and I dreamt I would own such a ball one day, somehow convinced that they fell to the ground like ripe fruit in the autumn. A ball full of smouldering voices.

The singing came from my left. A fine background noise, no more than a low hum with the sporadic crackle of electric charge. You had to cock your ears to hear it.

There was the source, a few yards from the sign, on both sides of the road, on an incline covered with dry stubbly grass: ten feet high, made of diamond-shaped wire mesh stretched tight between poles buried deep in the ground, splitting into a 'v' on top to form a roof of barbed wire – an electric fence that was audibly live. And, on closer inspection, not only parallel to the road. The fence made a right turn and cut through the forest. Roughly six yards of forest had been dug up on either side of the construction; only a fool would consider climbing a tree and having a go.

I stared nonplussed at the impressive edifice. Was it a nature reserve? A private estate? Hunting ground? It was certainly vast. There wasn't an end in sight, in the forest or on the road; the metal disappeared like a ruthless razorblade into three horizons at once. Spinechilling perfection.

Lying on the incline, half covered by the loose soil, I spotted a couple of rods, remnants from the construction. I kicked them first with the tip of my shoe to be sure they weren't electrified, wriggled one of them free and dragged it to the sign. The metal felt gritty, an earthen cold invaded the palms of my hands.

I lifted the rod and waved it aimlessly at first, as if trying to balance a rubber baton, but once accustomed to my new centre of gravity I rediscovered my equilibrium and was thus able to tinker with the overhanging branches.

The wooden fingers suffered bruising. Pale, stringy fibres emerged from beneath the bark, which turned mushy under my dull thumps. Leaves tore and fragments of green snowed to the ground. The sound of snapping wood and metal scraping metal grated against the roots of my teeth. Swallowing didn't help.

Little by little, lesion after lesion, letters were exposed. White, squared letters. The grip of the wooden claws had left them marbled, a seemingly very exclusive font, the sort you could only order from a few stationary stores worldwide. Panting, and with a rusty cramp in my arms, I finally lowered the rod.

FALL MILITARY BASE
CAMP X
THE GATEWAY
All I could do was stare at it.

But it still made me a tiny bit nervous, as if a Jeep could appear from the forest at any moment, thundering toward me, an armoured vehicle, decked out with powerful spotlights and soldiers on footboards with sturdy helmets and night-glasses who would surround me in no time, force me to my knees with stern, menacing commands and raised rifle butts, while one of them deftly lassoed my hands and tied them behind my back with a plastic noose that bit deeper into my wrists with every wriggle of resistance, then manhandled me into the trunk, a black hood over my head, my chest to the floor that smelled vaguely of rifle oil and soil, the ribbed sole of an army boot pressed between my shoulder blades, jiggling and jolting toward an unknown destination, to hollow sounding vaults deep under the ground, draged me on my knees and the points of my shoes over a shiny polished concrete floor, my underarms in the grip of two muscled claws, until I felt a needle penetrate my lower arm, only to wake up hours   days? – later, naked, shackled to a metal chair in a windowless room with a powerful desk lamp pointing at my face, eradicating every darkness, shining into my very brain, opening wide my mind like a carcass to allow nameless men with latex fingers to poke around in search of secrets, in search of the reason for my presence – my presence, which was already incriminating enough; why the interrogation, why would I be sitting here at all if I hadn't done something terrible, or was I trying to suggest that they, with all their secret cognisance, their clandestine omniscience, their information apparatus that has the whole world in its tentacles, that they, judges and executioners and gods all at once, had made a mistake, while the opposite was patently obvious, that my mere existence, or what remained of it – a shivering pile of trash, as irritating to them as a sliver of meat between their teeth – that my life was a massive, sickening misunderstanding, a vile superfluity that they should flush down the drain like a cockroach, and that they, and they alone, were in the right, and my only right, my final right to existence, was a confession, a mea culpa that couldn't save me, never, but could grant me at most a little dignity, that confessing everything was my only chance to finally, finally become what I always wanted to be: pure in the hour of my death.

No. None of that.

I stood there in the cold night air and stared at the sign, ran my eye one last time along the silver fence, turned and got into the car. Which started first time.

I saw the mist swirl in my rear-view mirror. The road in front of me. The barriers melted left and right into a glistening wall as I accelerated.

And I drove and I drove and drove.

No more.

Only the bead of warm sweat running down my left temple.

About Roderik Six's novel *Fall*

As if from nowhere, Doc, a young city doctor turns up in Fall, a small southern Canadian fishing town surrounded by a vast forest. He comes as if summoned: Lyndon, the old country doctor, has just died and Doc takes up residence in his grand house amidst the woods. On his rounds he gets to know a number of colourful figures: the insomniac sheriff Dwight who calls him at night to unfold Fall's history to him, the seductive Rose, who runs a brothel, and the young teacher Jonathan who would love to write a novel but doubts his talent.

But their stories soon come to resemble a confession – everyone seems to harbour a dark secret, and the doctor, too, must come clean about his past. Was his arrival in Fall a coincidence?

When he discovers a horrifying 8mm film clip in Lyndon's attic and women begin to disappear in Fall, the story takes a dark turn. What once seemed an idyllic spot now turns out to conceal a dark cancer.

In *Fall* Roderik Six goes armed with stylistic brilliance in search of the ultimate evil and what loneliness can do to a person. He proves himself a master of suggestion: his ironic narrative style and sparse, subtle use of language create the perfect atmosphere and tension.

TOM VAN DE VOORDE

Eleven Poems

TRANSLATED BY ASTRID ALBEN

ASKING SHIVA

with seaweed and surge

and roll across the agrarian plains
cloaked in foggy stars.

Bring me a battered fountain
a tether on a handful of horses,

the sun on a field of tiles
laid down in gold coloured sand. How

does the oil prompt the vase,
before a flower invents

its colour, before a dam wins its freedom.
All those friends, illuminated, sheltering

in the many nets. Count them and compute.
Ask her if she chose her name,

what it was: a few hewn out stones,
a roof, shored up against confusion,

a rising plain geographically naïve.
Maybe this was enough, Ahmadi,

to embroider the history of your land
with precious metals, necrologies

photo (c) Silvestar Vrijic

lying cheek by jowl, like conches
inventing additional limbs.

*

My postman asks me what
kingdom means in Hebrew

when I start to recapitulate
the pros and cons of serfdom to her

she bikes it down the hill
bellowing the last words of Hadrian

these are missing from the Britannica
at our next encounter

she points to a heap of stones
that has long been awaiting a tower.

TOM VAN DE VOORDE

*

I breakfast with Bertolt Brecht under the linden.
My plate shines yellow, his an orange glow.
The fried egg, burst open between us both,
no longer screams for attention:
thanks to the sun, thank heavens.
'Mein Lieber Freund', he casually remarks,
'Do you believe in Eastern Europe?'
The treetops a tightrope, each bole
a crammed tea ball. As we bid farewell
he gives me the recipe for a cocktail
long gone out of fashion, and asks me never
again to hammer at the truth. Danke schön I say,
for letting me hold him by the arms, ab und zu.

*

A gold panner illustrates
how to recognise a flight of stairs, spells

out the name of a mountain village
that was still a resort half a century ago,

and now said to be scattered with uncertain jetty's.
As soon as I grasped the latter,

she shaves her head bold,
not all, but the top left

above her forehead and jumps on a raft
of indeterminate provenance.

COMMUNIST AND SOCIALIST

When heroes share a love of fruitcake, their shoes will circle the
mud like palms. They esteem the truth of hunger and primal power
and allow architects to cross their arms. 'No longer than necessary,'
the older one remarks. The better-looking obliquely whispers what
I take to mean, 'Seek and forgive us our predilection for happiness
in arrears.' Gives thanks for that which is presented. When something waltzes past whose sound and status he wants to imitate, he
reminds his old friend of its metre. 'Yes you, who says *hmmpf* and
calls out *phiaow*.' A lack of something small, something subordinate,
like a clumsy book set aside to lisp from on one of those rare walks,
to sprinkle on yielding flowers.

PICNIC FOR STRANGERS

You recognise the boat by the butterfly scratched on the prow,
the bundle of sage, bruised when a buoy was cast overboard.

Blue with white reminds me of the course of the clouds
in a water barrel, waiting for villages and women

in summer. I now know what the doves mean
when they lay their clutch in a flag.

No one mentioned when the fleet would lay anchor.
Dreams blossom late with no visitors to expect.

Leave me behind, like you would a greeting at a garden gate,
paying no heed to who will hear it first.

Or take me to a door nearby twilight.
Show me what the sea recounts when it returns onto itself.

I embrace a wave and scream that I will change.
I utter what the fearful do, tormented by a star gleaming

in the surf. The song in the guitar of
the stranger is still to come.

Don't leave the house in a hurry.
Nothing forbids this place to wait.

The myth of the stranger is still to come,
while you can see those in hiding, fearing happiness.

How fearful will I be by the end of the song that my dream,
blue or white, will no longer come.

Perhaps the strangers lost their way
on their way to the picnic for strangers.

After Darwish

THE BEGINNING OF AN ISLAND

Before I stepped out of the bus station
and gazed to the left, I frisked
my memory for the little there is
to hold on to, let alone carry off.
The names of rivers, of extinct streets,
your hands, what I had promised them
when your eyes averted and mine fell
on a pattern of tiles that were no match
for the dragging gait of a long, slow exit.

FOUR QUESTIONS ABOUT A HAT

Bring a sail to glide
while you're in an operation

Welcome everyone
in your highest blue.

Cover a cluster with pigments
brush away the grass

because you don't want to wake up
to the propeller's hum.

Dance on singular legs
or a sensitive pair of scales.

And clear away the leaves
long before they get wet.

BLUDGEONING THEIR OWN SPECIES

Tick off something like Switzerland or Mercedes
and stay abreast of what inspires us

or send a postcard to train one's memory
in colour, often beaten by the wind.

We drink from jugs and see the houses
in toy-perspective. A worn out palm leaf

shimmers on chalk, fights off beloveds
and the logic of shell deposits.

FIKRY EL AZZOUZI

Drarrie in the Night

AN EXCERPT FROM THE NOVEL

TRANSLATED BY ANNA ASBURY

1

There are days when he puts me out like a bag of rubbish. Except people come round to collect the rubbish and they leave me on the curb. I can understand it, his fits of rage spring from an aggression disorder, he can't help that. You could compare my dad to a cat that has to catch mice or a mosquito that has to suck blood.

It's instinctive, the need to validate his dominance and show who's the man of the house.

Yes father, I know, in your house you're the man. No one doubts it. You'd marked out your territory long before I was born. But is it really necessary to chuck me out into the icy cold just because I slope in at eleven o'clock at night?

You say I'm a man? Then treat me like one. What's the big deal about eleven o'clock? Some people are at work at that time of day. Some are sitting down to a meal. Some are out clubbing. Some people are on their way to prayer.

Eleven o'clock is a good time to get home. If I'd been drunk, or high on coke, then I'd understand. Yeah, then you'd have the right to behead me. I'd hand you the knife myself.

Does he understand that his behaviour's not normal? Who sends an innocent son out into the night? Potentially fatal for a fifteen-year-old. Unless your name is Ayoub. And my name just happens to be Ayoub. Although everyone calls me Youb. Short and sweet, just like me.

Perhaps you see it differently, dear reader, but I'm convinced the dads in this retarded village get together in the mosque to confer on punishment. I can just picture it. One dad says, 'My son's grown

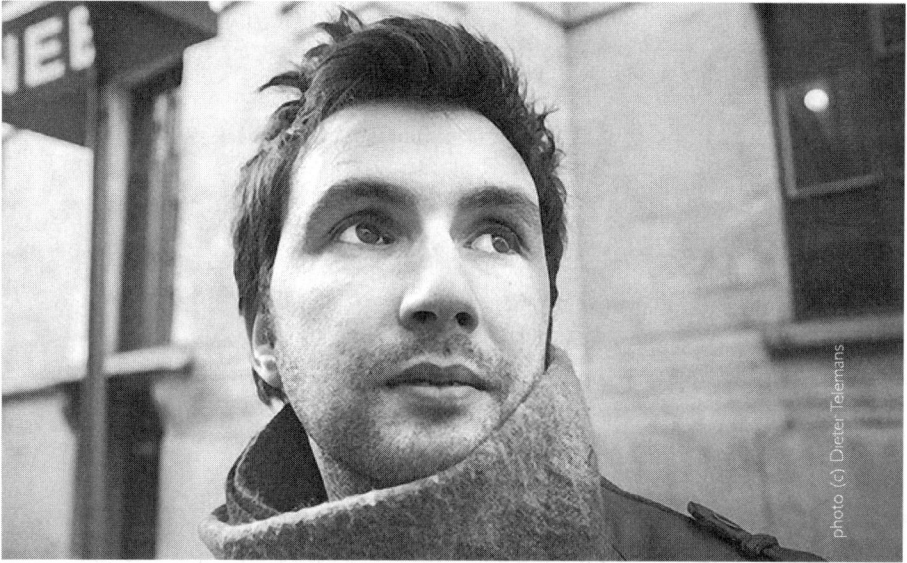

photo (c) Dieter Telemans

too big and strong for the belt. I'm beginning to feel I can't punish him respectably.'

'Throw him out,' the other replies. 'Show him whose house it is. Show him you and you alone are King Mohammed VI of the house. Let him taste the rain and the cold.'

All the other dads stand there fiddling with their beards and nodding approvingly. Perhaps they chink glasses of peppermint tea and sing a little song to boot: 'Throw them out, throw them out. Forget the warm, you little louts.'

I know, I'm singing a silly song. But really, you have to see them at it to know how silly the dads are. Well, anyway, I don't write songs and I'm not the person who should be educating dads. There are mirrors for that, and psychologists to explain their behaviour.

I have to walk nine hundred metres to the laundrette to see which of my friends' dads have told them to piss off too. That's the way it goes if you live in Waasdorp. Even if it's pretty much dead here, I still feel like I'm living in a zoo. With every step I take my ears ring with the cries of chimpanzees, the trumpeting of elephants and the hissing of snakes. The people are like animals driving you crazy, it's so stifling here. Still, I always take care how I walk. Round here you have to walk in style, with self-confidence, otherwise you're no more than an old man in search of his walking frame. Let me explain: you have to lean back a bit. Puff up your chest and swing your right arm.

Put your left hand in your pocket, that's just for wiping your arse. That's walking the Drarrie walk.

Am I the first one to get to the laundrette? I seriously hope I'm not going to have to sit here alone all night long. Last time I went and sat on the ironing board out of pure desperation. I fell asleep and only woke up the next morning. With a stiff neck, and broken back and a whole load of mosquito bites.

Since there's a chance I'll be here alone all night long, I've brought a notebook just in case. From now on I'm going to write up all my experiences whenever I'm chucked out. You might not know it yet, but I have a very interesting life and writing's not so difficult, at least not if you're a genius like me. The few books I've read are either dull as ditch water or unreadable. I can do way better. Not that writing is anything special. Why am I doing it then? Why do people smoke, if it kills you? Why do fat people eat fatty food? Why do parents beat their children? The answer is as simple as the question: it's stronger than you are.

I'll go ahead and sit in the corner. Just behind the ironing board. I can concentrate properly there. The cops won't see me and I won't be disturbed by passers-by who like to peek through the window.

You're probably wondering why we've picked a laundrette, aren't you? There's nothing open here in Waasdorp. You can hide away here for free. As soon as the sun sets, all the curtains and all the cafés close. Apart from Black Maria. That stays open. An old lady stands behind the bar, with silver-grey hair which was once black. She takes care of frustrated elderly people, offers them a listening ear, and maybe a good deal more. Old people might look innocent, but the older you get, the filthier your thoughts. I'm speaking from experience, as a child I was completely innocent in my head.

We're not welcome in Black Maria's place. I can understand Black Maria's perspective. We're a threat to her customers. We're young, good looking and we smell gorgeous. Old people are... where shall I start? Grey hair, nasal hair, ear hair, they smell funny and their only achievement in the day is a successful bowel movement. They're on their way to demented, so they don't know anymore whether they farted or the dog barked. Old people have bad teeth or no teeth, whereas mine are pearly white. Have you ever sat and talked with a toothless old person? I only have one word for it: 'Tfoe.'

I could go on all night about the elderly, but I'll stop there. Talking ill of the elderly is haram and I shouldn't waste time on it, they're as good as dead anyway.

Oh yeah, there's also a teahouse where Moroccans and other communities, apart from whites, drink tea and gossip, play dice and whatever other games they play. We Drarrie call teahouses like that not-for profits.

I'm not allowed to speak ill of my own community, but we Moroccans are the most tiresome, unreliable and perverse of the lot. But very occasionally you find an undiscovered pearl in that muckheap. A pearl named Ayoub.

We're not allowed inside the not-for-profit. Our mouths are too big, we get into fights with everyone and have no respect for our elders. What about respect? They might be ten years older, but it looks more like and they expect us to fall on our knees and kiss their hands. As far as I'm concerned the not-for-profit can get lost. It's more fun in the laundrette. You can get soft drinks, coffee and sweets from the machines. There's even a machine for bread, eggs and jam. Plus you don't get bothered by stupid men with ugly mugs and triple chins gazing lovingly at each other all day long while slurping tea.

The writing's not flowing, I can't concentrate. No need to worry, though, I'll have another go in a minute. What should I do in the meantime in this laundrette? My friends can't all be home watching TV like good boys.

'What shall I do?' I yell.

Play with my phone a bit? Way too dull. Crank out some push-ups? Way too tiring. I'm not as sporty as Fouad, he trains all day long. Oh yes, I'll send Fouad a message: Where are you? Am at the laundrette.

Fouad's parents won't let him in the house any more. Well, it's mainly his dad who won't let him in. His mum lets it happen and feels sad. That's the way it goes with mums. When Fouad's dad leaves the house, he dashes in for a shower, pulls on a fresh pair of boxers and stuffs some food in his mouth.

Fouad's been hanging around outside for several weeks now. He wanders the streets like a tramp. He doesn't really mind. I think he actually likes it. No more nagging, no fuss, just doing what you feel like. You don't have to justify yourself if you're not back by dark. It's the ultimate freedom.

It's just a question of time before the police drive by the laundrette and I have to piss off. Then I can wander round with Fouad, or Karim, or Maurice. Alone is alone. Although I sometimes feel lonelier in their company.

'Ewa Youb, kicked out again or what?' Karim laughs, suddenly wandering into the laundrette.

'No, I like it here and I really enjoy the view of the washing machines and driers.'

'What are you doing all hidden away back there? Were you wanking? Were you about to come? Ooo, did I disturb you? Shall I leave you alone and come back later?' Karim laughs loudly.

Okay, first let's clarify things, otherwise you won't be able to follow. Karim's real name is Kevin. Karim whose real name is Kevin is as white as a glass of milk on a lazy Sunday morning. He's the only whitey in our group. Why does he hang out with us? Because he feels good around us. Don't you ever dare call him Kevin, or he'll go completely mental. Karim's a minority among us, and without realising it, he adopts most of the customs of the majority. That's called integration. Let's call Karim a convert. He has all the characteristics of a convert. Sometimes he actually gets religious, starts praying, wears a djellaba in broad daylight and keeps on wagging his finger at us and telling us off. No, that's not true, he doesn't wag his finger, he sticks it right in our faces to clarify his point. Fortunately he doesn't keep it up very long, Drarries have far too much of a bad influence on him.

The problem with Karim is that he keeps on wanting to prove himself. He wants to be darker and more religious than we are. It doesn't look like it on the outside, but from inside he looks like a black man with a henna beard, a prayer cap, a djellaba and the latest pair of Nike Air Max trainers. He always wants to act smarter and make more trouble than us. And sometimes he goes too far. What am I saying? No, that's not true, Karim always goes too far. Like last week, when he went to the town hall to definitively change his name to Karim. The official asked him why he wanted to swap a nice name for an ugly one. Said he should be happy with the name his mother gave him. He should be proud of his background.

Karim, who has a short fuse, probably because of the integration, went berserk. Karim probably thought the official was calling his mother names. Or worse, that the official was asking for his mum's phone number. I don't know what goes on in those converts' heads.

The official must have had the thrashing of his life that day. Not that Karim wanted to murder him, but it came pretty close. Standing outside the town hall smoking a cigarette after the flogging, he was arrested by the police and spent a night in a cell. Next day he went back to the town hall to change his name. Just to show the official he wouldn't be broken. But the official was in hospital with his injuries, and a nice, pretty young lady was there instead. She told him that it's very difficult to change your name. And very expensive. If it were the other way round, changing Karim to Kevin, it'd be a piece of cake. And dirt cheap. Karim was overcome with shyness and her voice sent cold shivers down his spine. He thanked the young woman and left. In retrospect he terribly regretted not having asked for her number. Now I'm sure you have your thoughts on Karim. I have one word for him: moron.

Karim decides for himself when to leave the house. He's never kicked out. Fortunately for him he's not bothered by a dad, he only has a mum. His mum's not a hundred percent perfect, she's got an alcohol problem. Every evening she drowns herself in Duvel. Then she lies on the sofa all night gibbering. That's why Karim prefers to hang around outside in the evenings. That and wanting to show solidarity with us.

Secretly Karim fantasises about an invisible dad lecturing him. Secretly he fantasises about a dad who gives his mum a good hiding. That's what the drunken witch deserves. Don't look so surprised. They're not my words, they're Karim's. Do you know why Karim hangs out with us? Because he can kick back and be himself. Karim's not a hundred percent. I'm not a hundred percent. None of my friends are a hundred percent.

'What are you writing notes about? Don't you have time for me? Trying to show you're clever? Playing the intellectual. Wanna wear a hipster pair of glasses or something? What are you writing, is it about me? Write about me, I'm really interesting. Really someone should write a book about me. I've experienced a whole load of stuff. I'd do it myself, but I'm always too busy. Actually I can't stand words and all those letters stress me out and give me a headache,' shouts Karim.

I shrug and carry on writing. Delusions of grandeur, all my friends suffer from them.

'You know what I dreamt yesterday? I know it's strange, but I dreamt I ate my mum. In my dream my mum was still alive. She demanded I cut off her hands. Then I had to cook them in a pan with some onion and garlic. She said her hands mustn't be wasted, they had to be useful. In my dream the hands tasted really good and my mum couldn't open a can or hold a glass anymore. Perhaps that's the solution to her problem,' says Karim.

'Cutting her hands off? She can still use a straw and drink hands free.'

'Idiot, you always have to spoil it.'

'I don't understand why your mum needs to stop drinking. Be glad and enjoy your freedom.'

'Why did I bother telling my dream to a moron?' Karim sighs, looking outside and seeing a woman in a red coat walk by.

'Come on, let's follow her. I think she's drunk. You can see it from miles away,' says Karim.

'And then what? At most she'll piss her pants or get lost on her way home. I don't know what all those drunkards are up to. Anyway, according to you everyone's drunk at night, she could just be walking home.'

'Come on, we'll go ogle her a bit, have a bit of a laugh, a bit of rwina, then the night will be over,' says Karim.

'You want to scare her?'

'Yeah, that's a laugh, right? Maybe I'll touch her up a bit. Did you know some women fantasise about groping in a dark alley? Specially if it comes from a good looking young man. Yallah Youb, we'll make her dreams come true,' says Karim.

Women fantasising about being groped in dark alleys. I'd say he's a hundred percent right about that. As long as they're groped by Drarries.

I hesitate about going with him, but anything's better than sitting on a washing machine all night.

'First let me just note that Karim and I are going to give a woman with a red coat the fright of her life. Maybe we'll grab her bag, but probably not. Knowing Karim, he'd rather grab her bum, even if she'd prefer he didn't,' I say, writing busily in my notebook. I stop writing, shake my head and scrap the last sentence. Clearly I still have a lot to learn.

'Are you coming now?' shouts Karim.

I jump up and we go in search of her. In the distance we see a tall, slim woman walking along. We run towards her, stop five metres' away and saunter along behind her. Karim hisses. I join in. The woman doesn't turn round.

'What beautiful black boots she has. I bet they're really expensive. I can just smell the leather,' says Karim, sniffing loudly. 'Miss, what a beautiful red coat you have.'

There's a nervousness to the woman's pace now. We're like wolves, we can smell fear.

'What shiny brown hair that woman has. I'm sure it's not dyed. Her hair smells so good. Miss, could I smell your hair please,' asks Karim.

We're both sniggering away until I say, 'What long legs she has. Slim and muscular, as they should be. I think her red coat and black skirt go very well. I'm curious how the front of her looks. Hopefully it's as good as the back.'

'I'm shaking just thinking about it,' says Karim in a shaky voice.

The woman grips her little leather handbag tighter.

'What a beautiful little bag she has. Very stylish, I'm curious what's inside,' says Karim.

'It's a classy bag. Give the woman a clap for her class,' I shout.

'What, she's got the clap? That's filthy talk, I don't think she thinks much of you or your filthy talk. Leave her alone now Youb. No means no. But when I look at her bum. So beautiful, so big, so round and so alone,' sings Karim laughing at his own joke.

Suddenly we rush at the woman, overtake her and turn around. We look at her and she looks back at us, knees knocking and frightened eyes. With a broad smile Karim says, 'Pretty.'

'Very pretty, especially her red coat,' I say.

'Madam, what big eyes you have.'

'Madam, what a big mouth you have.'

'Madam, what big tits you have.'

'Madam, what a big bum you have.'

'Madam, what a big...'

Karim doesn't know what to say, so we stop and let the woman, who really isn't that pretty at all, walk on by.

You know what the look in her eye said? I'll tell you. She'd have liked to run into that dark boy on his own but wouldn't touch that toffee-nosed Belgian with a barge pole.

We go back to the laundrette.

'Did you have fun, then?'

'To be honest, no. Frightening women bores me. We're too old for it. I think we need to come up with something else to occupy ourselves,' Karim replies.

'Why didn't you grab her handbag? We had a chance then.'

'What did I just tell you? Are we twelve years old? Plus, I'm a good person,' says Karim.

In the laundrette Karim tells me about the Red Devils. He says Marc Wilmots should be sacked at last. Marc Wilmots doesn't have the head to coach Belgium. Too white and too worn out.

'Who's Marc Wilmots?' I lie.

'The Red Devils' coach. Don't you know anything? You're really not interested in anything. Write that down: I'm a writer who's not interested in anything.'

'Yes I am, I'm very interested in myself.'

'Haven't you ever wondered why all the management are white? In the Red Devils almost all the players are black, but the coach is white. Ever thought about that? No, you have a me-myself-and-I mentality. I'll explain it to you. Don't forget to write this in your little diary, Mr Look-how-clever-I-am-cos-I've-got-a-pen-in-my-hand. Like seeks out like. It's true of animals and it's true of people. That's the way the world works. Whites'll never put immigrants in top jobs. No, they're only allowed to play on the field like monkeys. Do you really think those footballers are that good? Okay, maybe they are good, but the main thing they need to be is stupid. Racists, we live in a world full of racists. Remember that when you watch a match. I refuse to support the Red Devils. When they get a black coach or a Muslim manager, I'll become a fan again,' says Karim.

'Tarnon, you're really talking rubbish, and your story's not even true. What are you doing with us? Like seeks out like? Shouldn't you be hanging out with white Flemish kids? Think of your future. Ever thought of hanging out with your own kind? That's the only way you're going to get top jobs and drive a big fat BMW. CEO Karim Van De Walle,' I say.

'Fuck top jobs, fuck my surname. Firstly, I've been through more dark times than you, so I'm way darker than you. Can you imagine what it's like growing up without a father? No, you're too stupid and egotistical for that. Secondly, I won't sell my soul, not to anyone. You'd give your own backside for a dürüm. And I'm pretty sure a dürüm would fit perfectly up your backside too. Thirdly, I may be a layabout, but you're a way bigger layabout, you just don't realise it.'

'You know what your problem is? You're jealous because you didn't have a dad to mistreat you when you were little,' I said.

Karim changes colour slightly and starts to stutter. He looks at me penetratingly for a few seconds and says, 'You know what I've just noticed? Why do they call themselves the Red Devils? Are they trying to promote Satan? Do they want us to support the devil? I should have known, the devil's everywhere and football's a sport that was invented for the devil.'

About Fikry El Azzouzi's novel *Drarrie in the Night*

In *Drarrie in the Night*, Fikry El Azzouzi describes a small group of young people who call themselves 'Drarrie' and populate the fringes of society. Ayoub is 15, a watcher rather than a doer. At night, in the village where he lives, he hangs out with his friends in the street, out of necessity, and chronicles their adventures in little notebooks. They are not the worst of the bunch, any of them, but they do behave like little ruffians. Fouad, who is being sponsored by a rich white man to do body-building with banned substances, Maurice, half Belgian and half Ivorian, and Karim, who is actually called Kevin and is white, but feels more at home amongst the 'drarrie' as a Muslim.

They meet up in the evening hours to beat the boredom and armour themselves in their aversion of the society around them. The lads are, more than anything, themselves and have given up communicating with the world around them. Only one way seems open to them: the path of self-destruction.

What begins as an entertaining picaresque novel slowly turns into a chilling story of radicalisation when one of the boys decides to leave Flanders to become a martyr . . . With a deft pen and biting humour, Fikry El Azzouzi sketches a picture of a generation of young people who are looking for meaning and identity in our society. He opens up a world that is close at hand, but unfortunately unknown to many.

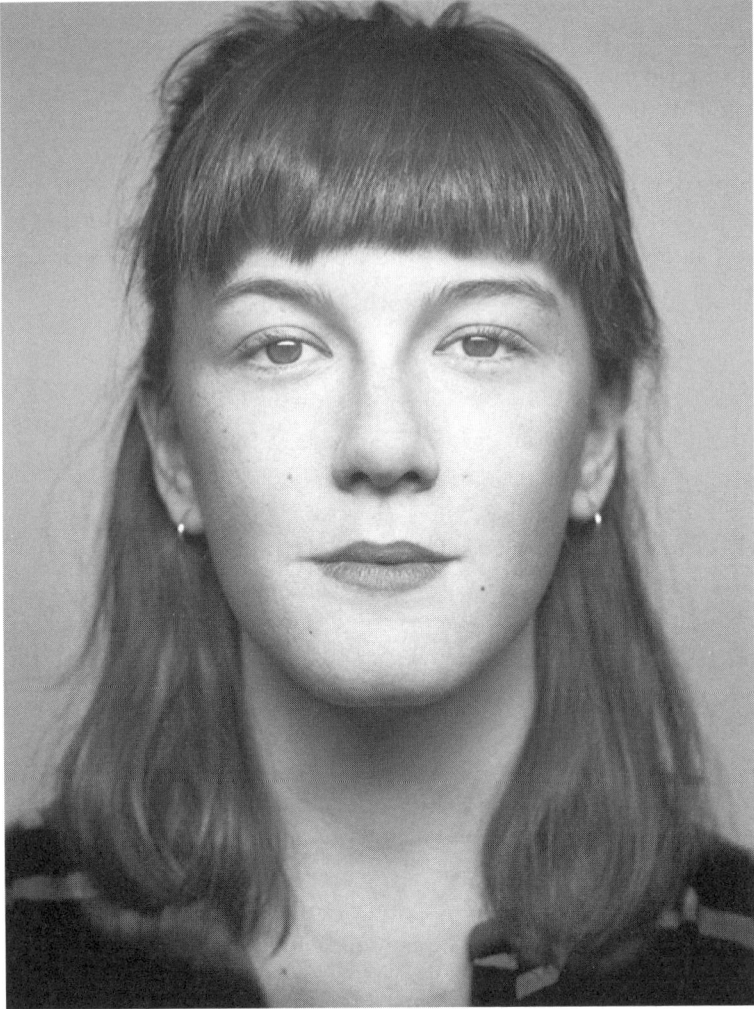

CHARLOTTE VAN DEN BROECK

Five Poems

TRANSLATED BY ASTRID ALBEN

BUCHAREST

Some places are so small
they'd fit on the tip of a finger.
I try to point at where everything was
but I can barely remember.

Among the rubble of forgetting stands
my grandfather's bookcase and that Sunday afternoon
when we read the atlas together, his finger
resting on the capital of Romania.

'A smashing bunch of slags they had,' he said
and I thought a slag was some sort of Eiffel Tower
and resented him for never bringing me back a miniature version.

Later I learned that borders and grandfathers are relative.
Only that afternoon is marked in the atlas
by raised alphabet letters, as the afternoon
when I still saw in him the most perfect guide.

SISJÖN

A grandfather and child stand naked at the edge of the lake.
We decide that this is natural,
stare politely at our toes whilst stepping out of our clothes.

We force our cheeks into a smile.
One glance wipes away the innocence of my bathing suit.
This is how we glide into the water, impish.

We swim across the lake, breaststroke
feels strange without the contours of a swimming pool.
I talk about my mother's breasts floating on the water in the bath.
How they seemingly contradicted gravity.

We smoke ciggies on top of your sleeping bag, for me a first.
My gums feel like a dried apricot stone,
but I tell him it tastes all right.

In the morning the sun burns us out of our tent,
where we find the dead chick.
Whatever it was, it was defenceless.

VÄXJÖ

There's a lightness in the air that wrings.
We look like kids washed up in the corner
of the playroom, fists bawling on the mat,
screaming that their bodies are bursting at the seams.

At noon we stare into the sun with bulging chameleon eyes,
the world smudged in coarse grease pencil lines.
There's no noticeable difference between the hand and the table
just the transition of matter.

In the wavering image of magnified pixels
a girl's hair sways in long ponytails, hair
that isn't yet a trump card but a burden when she plays.
When she walks the tails swish like whips.

A lethargy weighs everything down:
more mass on top of the same surface area
causing things to tumble off somewhere
along the margins of the world.

There's a lightness here that wrings.
As if it's all just a marble alley
a way from up to down
until someone lifts us up again.

HVANNADALSHNÚKUR

Fingertips, suction pads, don't fall asleep now
if you don't fall asleep now we will talk now
we can talk, here, on top of these sheets
talk about the pale hills across the water,
the sods of grass where we sat
where we hadn't sat together yet, summers
we experienced separately, the lighter of our hair
and the longer of the days, here, on top of these sheets

make sure you don't break now, the scorpions in my bookcase
are travelling tonight, it's safe now, the heat
on the windows, the steam from your stories, it's almost
morning on top of these sheets, a final hour, here
in my languid loins, stay, talk a little now
in the languidness of my loins

about: bellybuttons, the silly season, talk a distant land in my ears
the branches on sturdy trees lining the sound of the words
here, fevered dreams, here, on top of these sheets knurs for hands
and bowls of thirst, white lilies in the living room, the walls
long-forgotten blueprints, the innocence of rain worms
in a child's mouth, we can talk here, on top of these sheets.

BULLS HEAD

Ever since I was born an enormous bulls head rages
in my mother's belly. It's on a rampage in her empty womb

creating scars in the fallow mother. Sometimes
she doesn't quite recognise me, which is troubling

because at one time I fitted inside her perfectly. Luckily,
according to the astronomical constellation of Cancer

I'm pleasure seeking, reliable and creative. She finds this
    consoling,
an article of faith connecting amniotic fluid to the universe.

Whenever we had chicory baked with gammon, I'd get the crust
    of cheese.
All of it. Because I'd asked for it.

The love I know is dished up from a casserole,
the two extra helpings on a full plate
that second biscuit hidden in the yellow pud.
This is a typical feature of motherly conduct:

'Stuffing ones young'.
In exchange for the void I left in her, she wanted me full and
    round.

Then came the morning I announced the arrival of two small
    breasts.
The news broke her spirit for days.

Eventually she handed me a bra,
emblazoned with Hello Kitty.

Deep inside her belly raged the snorting bulls head.
A void is emptiness only when nothing else will fit.
Gradually we fossilised into two separate creatures.
We can no longer tell

who became the insect and who
turned into amber.

From the poet's debut collection *Kameleon* (Chameleon),
published by De Arbeiderspers, Amsterdam / Antwerpen, 2015

Laura Fererri reviews

No Knives in the Kitchens of this City
by Khaled Khalifa

Translated by Leri Price
Published by Hoopoe Fiction (AUC Press)
15 October 2016, ISBN: 9789774167812,
pbk, $17.95 / £9.99 / LE120

The challenge of family

And broken dreams are the main themes of Khaled Khalifa's latest novel, *No Knives in the Kitchens of this City*, which tells the story of the decline of a Syrian family over a period of sixty years. There are no winners in a country where freedom is limited not only by the regime, but also by the fear of other people's judgement.

Through the eyes of the narrator, the reader gets to know the story of Sawsan and Rashid, the narrator's siblings, and their mother and uncle, Nizar. Despite the complexity of the narration, which jumps continuously back and forth in time, the novel is an enjoyable reading which keeps the reader entertained till the end.

No Knives in the Kitchens of this City is Khaled Khalifa's fourth novel. It was awarded the Naguib Mahfouz Medal for Literature in 2013 and was shortlisted for the International Prize for Arabic Fiction in 2014. Like Khalifa's previous novel, *In Praise of Hatred*, *No Knives in the Kitchens of this City* has been beautifully translated by Leri Price.

The beginning of the story makes immediately clear that the matriarch of the family is a defeated character. She has challenged her family and renounced her social status to marry a man from a lower class who, after having four children with her, abandoned the family to move to America with another woman. She, however, does not seem to be particularly upset by this abandonment and believes that soon she will marry another man. On the other hand, what causes her a strong feeling of shame is having a disabled daughter, Suad, whom she hides away from the sight of her neighbours, afraid of their judgement. She waits for the young girl to die to be released from the shame and be able to put the pieces of her life back together. Contrary to her expectations, Suad's death only contributes to the destruction of the family. Her other children, Sawsan, Rashid and the narrator, who were very fond of Suad, are extremely affected by her death and resent their mother for her behaviour towards the poor girl. The family links become weaker by the day, while the mother sinks into dementia, becoming everything she has always been ashamed of.

Sawsan, the rebel and beautiful sister of the narrator, joins the paratroopers and starts working as an informant for the regime. After falling in love with an officer, Munzir, she leaves for Dubai with him, hoping to become his wife. However, Munzir chooses to marry another woman and Sawsan has to return to Aleppo. Once back in Syria, she starts regretting her past, feeling shame for ruining the lives of many of her fellow students when working as an informant, and therefore decides to look for purification by living a more modest and secluded life.

Rashid, a talented musician, is at first glance the only character who has a chance of succeeding in life. He plays in his uncle's band and lives a quiet life until the day he becomes involved with a fundamentalist group and leaves Syria to fight against the Americans in Iraq. Rashid sees in martyrdom the meaning of life and is eager to die for his faith and reach heaven. However, when the Americans capture him, afraid of being tortured, he declares a fake Christian identity and manages to escape. Back in Syria, Rashid is haunted by the shame of having denied his faith to save his life.

Nizar, the narrator's gay uncle, is the only character whose defeat is not caused by his own choice but by the judgment of a society that has yet to understand and accept homosexuality. In his youth, after spending some time in jail accused of sodomy by his own family, he had moved to Beirut and enjoyed the relative freedom homosexuals had in Lebanon. Forced to return to Syria after running out of money and struggling to pursue his music career in Beirut, he moves back to Aleppo where he becomes a famous musician. Despite his success,

WINNER OF THE NAGUIB MAHFOUZ
MEDAL FOR LITERATURE

No Knives
in the
Kitchens
of This City

A NOVEL

"One of the rising stars of Arab fiction"
NEW YORK TIMES

Khaled Khalifa

Translated by Leri Price

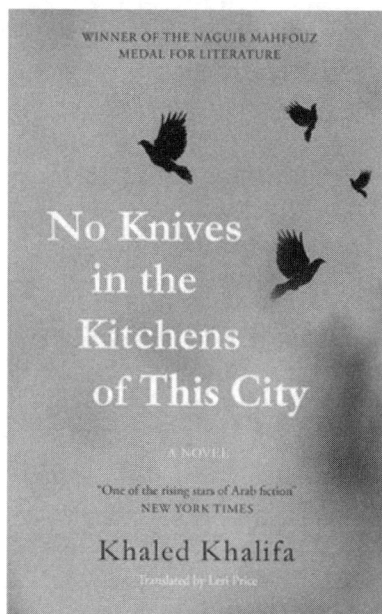

he is unable to live the life he desires and dedicates most of his time to helping his sister and her family.

Khaled Khalifa unfolds the events of this story with incredible talent, dealing with delicate topics, such as homosexuality and mental illness, with great sensitivity.

I particularly enjoyed the way he develops the characters. On the one hand, there are Sawsan and Nizar, extremely well constructed to the point that their behaviour can never be questioned because it mirrors perfectly their personalities. On the other hand, there is Rashid and the mother, whose personalities are more blurred, leaving the reader wondering the reasons behind some of their choices. Little is known about the unnamed narrator. He gives almost no detail about his life and refrains from any comment about the story he narrates, acting as a mere spectator.

Disguised under the mask of fiction, there is a clear intent by the author to express his political opinion towards the regime and the Leader, whose name and party are never openly mentioned. Khalifa does so through the words of the mother of the narrator for whom living under the regime is as if she is lacking the air to breathe, and through the description of the difficult life of Aleppo's population. This culminates with the scene that gives the book its title, the scene in which a desperate man sets his family on fire to spare them the suffering of starvation, and then kills himself with a kitchen knife.

After more than five years from the outbreak of the Syrian war and the ensuing refugee crisis, *No Knives in the Kitchens of this City* is a much needed work of literature, which helps the foreign reader understand the suffering of the Syrian people without aiming at cheap emotional effect, but providing food for thought and an invitation to be ever more compassionate.

Samira Kawar reviews

The Dove's Necklace
by Raja Alem

Translated by Katherine Halls
and Adam Talib

Published by Overlook Books (USA),
Duckworth (UK), both June 2016.
USA: ISBN 9781590208984, 480pp, $29.95
UK: ISBN 9780715645864, 544pp, £18.99

Giving a home to ancient Mecca

Raja Alem's novel, *The Dove's Necklace*, is a work of brilliant virtuosity that packs several narratives and intertwining themes into a single framework. The original Arabic version won her the International Prize for Arabic Fiction in 2011. The novel's English translation, adeptly accomplished by Katharine Halls and Adam Talib, was published earlier this year.

The plot is highly complex and nuanced. Alem warns the reader at the very outset not to expect a revelation of certainties. "The only thing you can know for certain in this entire book is where the body was found: the Lane of Many Heads, a narrow alley with many heads," says Alem in the novel's opening sentence. And she is as good as her word.

Although the plot initially focuses on the efforts of a detective by the name of Nasser to identify the corpse of a young woman that mysteriously appears in the alley and find her killer, it gradually morphs into a spiritual journey of self-discovery for Nasser and the novel's other main characters, both men and women.

Alem gives a clue to the main theme of her novel by making the Lane of Many Heads its first main narrator, and endowing it with a character. As the meandering plot unfolds and breaks up into several narratives, it becomes apparent that the alley's many heads are also the novel's main characters, and the alley is emblematic of the entire

ancient city of Mecca, which has been systematically destroyed to make way for commer-
cialised modernity.

During a question and answer session in
London in August to mark the launch of the
novel's English translation, Alem revealed that
the body "appeared" in the novel, which took
five years to complete, after she had written
a quarter of it. The dead young woman "could
be anyone, the city itself," she says. It is a
metaphor for the death of old Mecca and its
traditions, and an attempt to document the
erasure of the city, of which Alem is a native,
to make way for gleaming, ultra-modern towers around the Muslim holy places in Mecca
and Medina. The destruction of the centuries-
old quarters of the city – represented in the novel by the Lane of
Many Heads and some of the buildings in the mountains around
Mecca – slowly unfolds as a grotesque crime of cultural, and even
religious vandalism. The spiritual and the traditional essence of the
city – represented by some of the novel's main characters, particularly the young historian and writer, Yousef, and the photographer
and son of the alley's Imam, Muaz – fight a losing battle against an
increasingly nightmarish modern and materialistic ethos. The futur-
istic, surreal and highly symbolic vision of gleaming towers that
emerges towards the end of the novel of what Mecca might look like
as the greed-fuelled real estate boom reaches its logical conclusion
evokes Aldous Huxley's *Brave New World*, although that narrative is
one-dimensional compared to *The Dove's Necklace*.

"Now I do not know Mecca, it has disappeared. Now I can only
find it in my book. I gave refuge to the city in my book," says Alem.
"I felt like a kind of custodian of the city and what it was: not only a
city of God, but also a city of man."

Yet the book is not merely set in the physical city of Mecca. The
city itself transcends its physical location to gain a new existence in
a spiritual realm that is independent of time and place.

The Dove's Necklace also chronicles the journeys of self-discovery
that its main young characters undertake as they seek to break out
of the confines of their austere misogynistic society, helped by the

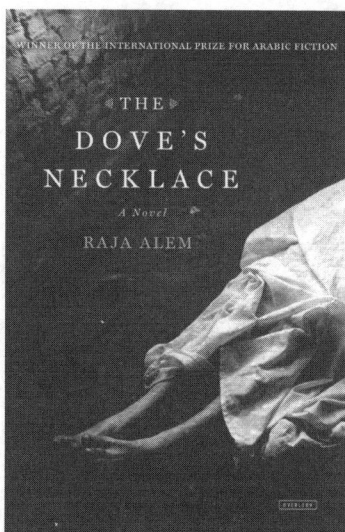

Raja Alem

tools of globalisation, such as the internet, email and travel abroad, all of which facilitate inter-cultural communication and exchange. Although the novel is not autobiographical, this sense of global interconnectedness is reflected in Alem's own experience. "I think of myself as a universal citizen," she says. The internet's ability to make "distances disappear" will "create more and more international citizens".

The Dove's Necklace is also a rich tapestry of interwoven traditions, customs, history, ancient beliefs and even myths. Although the characters, particularly the female ones such as Aisha and Azza, are victims, they also come across as strong women who exercise their own choices within the confines of the restrictions surrounding them. The alley's young men are also victims, and struggle in their own way to attain intellectual and spiritual freedom.

The long passages of introspective thought that the characters undertake are outward looking as well as inward looking, and often flow as a stream of consciousness. Alem says, "The moment I touch a keyboard, things happen. Things rush through me as though I were a medium."

The reflections of the characters are so frank and intimate that Alem was initially unable to write them in Arabic, resorting instead to writing and exploring them in draft form in English, before rendering them into Arabic.

"You feel the pain of the people. I still cannot read the book," says Alem. The emails of Aisha, one of two main female characters in the novel, to her German lover "reveal the pain of many women," she adds.

The Dove's Necklace is by no means an easy read, and requires focus and concentration. But the effort is well worth it.

Becki Maddock reviews
The Longing of the Dervish
by Hammour Ziada
Translated by Jonathan Wright
Published by Hoopoe Fiction (AUC Press),
September 2016
ISBN: 9789774167881, pbk, 288pp, $18.95 /
£9.99 / LE120

An impossible love

The *Longing of the Dervish* is an enchanting, poetic novel by Sudanese author Hammour Ziada. It exemplifies what Ziada has called "the Sudanese style", which he describes as "full of poeticism, in addition to the world the Sudanese culture belongs to, where African and Arab cultures mix". The Award Committee of the Naguib Mahfouz Medal for Literature described the novel as "an intricate love story of a Sudanese slave in the world of the Mahdist movement in nineteenth-century Sudan".

Born in Omdurman, Sudan, in 1977, Hammour Ziada is currently working as a journalist based in Cairo, Egypt. He is the author of two novels and two collections of short stories His first novel, *Al-Kunj* was published in 2010. The upheavals of the 2011 Arab uprisings and their aftermath distracted Cairo-based Ziada from completing his second.

He has said that he would often feel unsatisfied with his work and stop writing. Nevertheless, his second novel, *Shawq al-Darwish* (The Longing of the Dervish), was completed and published in 2014. It won the Naguib Mahfouz Medal for Literature and was longlisted for the 2015 International Prize for Arabic Fiction. The Mahfouz Medal judges praised not only the author's 'wide-ranging palette of characters and events' but also the range and dexterity of Ziada's writing.

The Longing of the Dervish is an unconventional love story, set in 19th century Sudan against a background of war, religious fervour and political turmoil. It explores a significant moment in Sudanese history, tracing the rise and fall of the Mahdist state in Sudan. The

Hammour Ziada

novel opens with the fall of Khartoum, the defeat of the Mahdist army, and the release of former slave Bakhit Mandil from prison. We learn that Bakhit was a fighter in the Mahdist army and is set on avenging the killing of his beloved Theodora. This is not a plot-spoiler. Theodora is already dead at the start of the novel. Through multi-layered analepsis and prolepsis Ziada gradually fills in Theodora and Bakhit's back stories, revealing to the reader, little by little, how they arrived at their fates, against the backdrop of the chaotic history of late 19th century Sudan, which is reflected in the novel's disordered broken time sequence. The chaotic time sequence of the novel evokes the chaos and uncertainty of the era it describes. Ziada has explained his conscious choice of this narration style, noting that 'If the novel was written in a classic cumulative style, maybe it would have been just a Sudanese version of *The Count of Monte Cristo* or any other universal novel about vengeance and impossible affection.'

Ziada employs multiple modes of discourse to tell the story of tragic hero Bakhit Mandil's hopeless love and quest for revenge. Narratives, from the viewpoint of various protagonists, are combined with poetry, songs, historical documents and Qur'anic and Biblical verses, and woven into a thought-provoking reflection on prejudice, freedom, and faith. Bakhit, Theodora and Hassan al-Jerifawi, another ex-Mahdist fighter, all question their faith and the deeds it has led them to do. Hassan asks himself: "Aren't they infidels? Aren't we believers?"

Bakhit's beloved Theodora is an Egyptian of Greek origin, who travels, as part of a group of missionaries, from her home in Alexandria, across the desert to Sudan, where she is caught up in the political power struggles between the British, Egyptians, Turks and Mahdists. Through Theodora, Ziada takes us inside the colonial mind-set, demonstrating the inherent sense of superiority and difference. On the journey to Sudan, Theodora asks Father Pavlos "Do the blacks smell as horrible as they look?" In a nod to orientalism, Theodora exoticises her desert journey, imagining herself to be a princess from *The Thousand and One Nights*. She contrasts her own "civilized world" with the "blackness" and savagery of Sudan, although she does recognise that "the Europeans don't set a good example for how Christians or civilized people should be". Although Ziada uses the Theodora character to exemplify many of the negative aspects of the colonial project, she is not an unsympathetic figure, rather a victim of her circumstances. She says of Bakhit: "If only he hadn't been black." When Hortensia, another nun, does not understand Theodora's friendship with Bakhit, saying "He's just a savage", Theodora assures her: "He's not like the others." The fear and suspicion are mutual. Sudanese Merisila states: "That Christian girl is a devil", while her countryman Idris remarks: "All white people are mad!"

Ziada's human exploration of the East-West encounter recalls Tayeb Salih's *Season of Migration to the North* in its portrayal of the inherent assumptions and prejudices on both sides of the colonial encounter. Ziada dissects the complexities of many encounters, depicting a world that is far from black and white. Followers of the Mahdi kill, rape and enslave in the name of God, but they had come initially as saviours to free people from injustices perpetrated by Turkish and British colonisers. Ziada reminds us that all people can be capable of kindness or savagery, loyalty or betrayal.

The love story is the driving force of Ziada's historical narrative, which explores sobering themes such as slavery, imprisonment, religious hypocrisy, and racism. There is a contradiction between the beauty of the novel's narrative and the ugly events it describes. Ziada takes us back to a bygone era, showing us the human side of Sudan's history. And as the Mahfouz Medal Committee accurately observed, Ziada's novel "is a powerful statement on the current scene in the region where religious extremism is causing havoc".

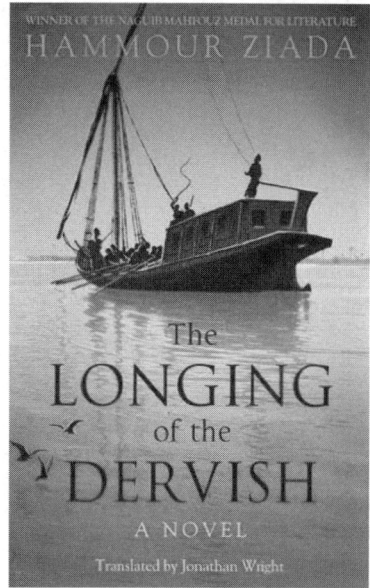

Peter Clark reviews

Sonallah Ibrahim, Rebel with a Pen
by Paul Starkey

Published by Edinburgh University Press, 2016.
ISBN 9780748641321, hbk, 248pp, £70.

A committed observer

The Edinburgh Studies in Modern Arabic Literature has a mouth-watering and mind-stimulating list of current and forthcoming publications. This is the only one in their current list to focus on one writer, Sonallah Ibrahim, now in his late seventies who has produced fourteen novels – which is, as Paul Starkey notes, about one every four years of his adult life. Six of those fourteen are available in English translation. Denys Johnson-Davies was his first translator into English, and that was forty-five years ago. The other translations into English have all been from the present century. But his work has also been translated into half a dozen other European languages.

Paul Starkey gives us a comprehensive introduction to a writer who is very much of the "Sixties" generation. An enthusiast for the July 1952 Revolution and then, for five years, a prisoner in one of Nasser's prisons, he shared the disillusion of many of his generation after the June 1967 war with Israel. He has been a detached but committed (if that is not too much of a contradiction) observer of the contemporary scene in Egypt and the Arab world. Detached, insofar as he avoided being a campaigning journalist but has retained a clear eye for nuances of bureaucracy or the complexities of human relations. Committed, insofar as he has retained the positive, secular, hu-

manitarian and open atti-
tudes of the 1960s. In 2003
he publicly refused the award
of the 100,000 Egyptian
pound prize offered by the
Egyptian Supreme Council
for Culture, with the words:
"I publicly decline the prize
because it is awarded by a
government that, in my opinion, lacks the credibility of
bestowing it." This was quite
a stand, for one who lived in
modest circumstances. He
was a full-time writer, and
there were personal risks for
dissidents.

Each of Sonallah Ibrahim's
works are analysed and com-
pared: the publication and translation history, the plot and an analysis
of the work. Certain themes are recurrent. He was acute in observ-
ing corruption, hypocrisy and sexual deviation. In later years he
recorded the ubiquitous and corrosive nature of globalisation.

Although Sonallah Ibrahim was very much a Cairene, he wrote several novels based outside Egypt. He is unusual as an Arab writer in
writing about other Arab countries but these other Arab countries –
Lebanon and Oman, for example, are seen through the eyes of a visiting Egyptian. In preparing the works that are located outside his
familiar Cairo he has researched the background. Most of his novels
are written in the first person and often that first person has features
– age and class – that echo Sonallah Ibrahim himself. One recurrent
character, Professor Shukri, appears in later novels, as a participant
at a conference in France and as a visiting professor in California,
roles that have been undertaken by Sonallah Ibrahim himself.

His conscientious craftsmanship and his integrity stand out. Paul
Starkey makes a convincing case that he is a writer whose work will
long survive the political and cultural turmoil that Egypt has recently
suffered.

Paul Blezard reviews

The Return: Fathers, Sons and the Land In Between

by Hisham Matar

Published by Viking, 30 June 2016.
ISBN: 978-0670923335, hbk, 288pp
£14.99 / $15.72, Kindle edition £9.99

An intimately personal tale

D o you remember 2006? It was the year that a seven-ton Northern Bottlenose whale swam up the River Thames, Australian naturalist Steve Irwin died after being pierced by a stingray barb and a hitherto unknown writer published an astonishing work that entered the shortlist for the MAN Booker Prize and the Guardian First Book Award. It went on to win the 2007 Commonwealth Writers' Prize Best First Book award for Europe and South Asia, the 2007 Royal Society of Literature Ondaatje Prize, the 2007 Premio Gregor von Rezzori, the Italian Premio Internazionale Flaiano and the inaugural Arab American Book Award. It clearly heralded a literary voice that was at once elegant, poetic and insightful and went on to be translated into some 28 languages.

The title of the book was *In the Country of Men*, and its author, Hisham Matar, received accolades aplenty from world renowned authors for his vivid and affecting depiction of life for ordinary residents as they try to survive in Libya under the terror of Qaddafi's regime. It very quickly became clear that a new star had exploded into being to illuminate the literary firmament.

Wind the clock forward to the present day and all the promise and potential of ten years ago is confirmed with Matar's latest, an intimately personal tale that eschews the novel in favour of the memoir and in so doing weaves a gripping, thriller-like tension through its strands of captivating revelation and endearing meditations on the emotional landscape where geo-politics and revolution meet family relationships.

In March 1990, Hisham's father, Jaballa Matar, a former soldier, diplomat, businessman and latterly one of the more prominent figures opposing Qaddafi's tyrannic rule, was kidnapped from the family's Cairo flat and delivered to Abu Salim prison, Qaddafi's house of horror in Tripoli, notorious for human rights abuses and the 1996 mass execution of some 1,270 prisoners that featured in journalist Lindsey Hilsum's excellent book *Sandstorm*. Matar writes:

". . . from prisoner testimonies that I've been able to gather with the help of Amnesty International, Human Rights Watch and the Swiss NGO TRIAL, we know that Father was in Abu Salim at least from March 1990 to April 1996, when he was moved from his cell and taken to another secret wing in the same prison, moved to another prison or executed."

This calm outlining of events belies the fear and pain that Matar elegantly explores throughout the story. His thoughtful analysis of events and of his feelings is as touching when describing his family's extended exile from Libya in London, Paris, New York, Cairo and Nairobi as it is affecting in his explanations of the profound impact his father's abduction and incarceration had on him and his family.

But for all its outlining of the death and deprivation of late 20th century Libya and the respectful admiration of heroic resistance and revolutionary activists, this is more than merely a bleak account of the slow death of a nation and a son's quest for the truth about his father's disappearance.

Matar is never better than when describing, with sensory delight, the quotidian rituals of family and Libyan life. Meals of pomegranate salads, the selection of the perfect olive oil, nutmeg or the plumpest pigeon by his mother, give way to aunts making sugar and orange blossom syrup and Matar's realisation that it is for the depilation of arms and legs rather than for consumption.

Light and air is also a recurring motif throughout, from the blue grey palette of London via the moist pine fragrance of a Cote D'Azur beach to the "bright as the skin of an orange" evening glow of Benghazi. But always he draws back to a darker scene. The waxy orange blossom syrup becomes the yellowed, disinfected skin in a photograph of a dead cousin, shot in Tripoli. Sunlight reminds him only of

Hisham Matar

the darkness of his father's cell in Abu Salim. Any fleeting joy or pleasure becomes tempered by Matar's sense of loss, of what could have been. A scene in New York where a crawl space beneath a sidewalk grating that gives Matar a shockingly visceral sense of his father's incarceration is profoundly affecting.

The third act is an account of a son's dogged, tenacious quest to find the truth. To determine if his father is alive or, if not, how and when his death occurred. With cloak and dagger style meetings with Seif Qaddafi, frustratingly endless calls upon the British Government for assistance, false leads, well meaning assistance from former Abu Salim captives and countless letters and emails to NGOs and governments, Matar leaves no lead unchecked. It is as compelling to read as it must have been painful to write.

In the final analysis, *The Return* is a memoir like no other. It is a love letter from a son to an adored father who taught him to "ride a horse, shoot a rifle and swim", who taught him to give "so discreetly that 'your left hand does not know what the right hand has done'". It is a hymn of celebration to all those who fight for truth and freedom, an elegy for those who perish for a just cause and a soaring, compelling example of the power of literature to vanquish the dark shadows of evil tyranny. But above all it is a noble and humane response to an awful episode, one that a reader can love and admire, one that would make any father supremely proud of his son.

Olivia Snaije reviews

About My Mother
by Tahar Ben Jelloun

translated by Ros Schwartz and
Lulu Norman

Published by Telegram (UK), July 2016
ISBN: 9781846592010
eISBN: 9781846592034
£8.99 / US $16.95, pbk, 288pp.

Sons and mothers

Tahar Ben Jelloun's book, *About My Mother*, out July 2016 in English for the first time, was published eight years ago in its original French. In a recent interview with the author, he said it was a book that had accompanied him over time because readers had often spoken to him about it in the context of their own ageing parents.

Although *About My Mother* is a fictional account of a son accompanying his mother as she makes her way towards death, it is, of course, inspired by Ben Jelloun's own relationship with his mother and her last moments.

"My mother was very modest and didn't tell me about many things, so I reinvented her life," said Ben Jelloun.

The narrative voices in *About my Mother* alternate between the son's and his mother's as she recalls moments from her younger self. She remembers being a beautiful young girl in the hammam with her own mother, when another woman approaches them to arrange a marriage with her son. Women have always played a central role in Ben Jelloun's work, and here, the themes of modesty and sexuality are ever present.

"Women from that era were completely submissive and I had to guess what they said to each other," said Ben Jelloun. However, "I was a child who was ill very often, so I was there in a corner and I could observe and listen to women when they were alone. They would talk about sex sometimes."

Ben Jelloun describes a joyful scene, which he says is true, in which the women of the house are baking and joking with each other; his aunt, known for her audacity, makes a cake in the shape of a penis and the women fight over who will eat it. The boy amidst the women, is reminiscent of a 1990 Tunisian film called *Halfalouine*, child of the terraces, about a young boy's life in the warm intimacy of the women's world, and his transition into the men's world when he reaches puberty.

Ben Jelloun also takes on his mother's sexuality – no easy feat – as well as intimate details about her, which contribute to the strength of his descriptions about the depth of their relationship. He describes the magnificence of her breasts that he knew as a child, and how he would have preferred not to catch a glimpse of her "withered, emptied, flabby skin" as a doctor examines her. He contrasts his mother's difference in attitude towards ageing with the European mother of one of his friends, Roland – at the same age as his mother, she is independent and active. Roland is "the Westerner" in all his splendour,

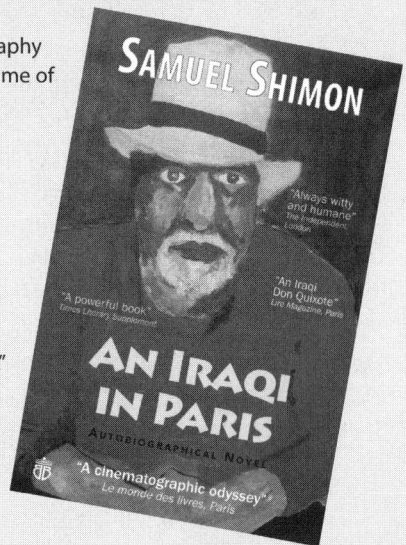

Tahar Ben Jelloun

an individual independent from his mother and for whom her death is something inevitable and expected, while in Morocco, said Ben Jelloun, "we are not separate from our parents. The tie between parents and their children is very strong; it's almost a religion."

But Ben Jelloun doesn't only talk about his mother — he also broaches the subject of observance, and faith. Both his parents were tolerant and felt their children's relationship with God was their private business, but his father was a free thinker who also had many doubts. Ben Jelloun describes a scene in which, as a child during the winter, he had to fetch freezing water from a well for washing. His father summons him and his brother and says: "Prayer is one of the five pillars of Islam. You must pray five times a day. You can even say all five at the end of the day. It's not a punishment. If you don't feel the need to pray, then don't pray. But don't pretend, there's no point."

This too was a real memory, said Ben Jelloun, and after his conversation with his father: "I was completely liberated."

In this relatively slim book, Ben Jelloun manages to insert reflections on many aspects of Moroccan culture, with the inviolable relationship between parents and children at its core, at once respectful and stifling, and a man's relationship with his mother which begins in all innocence and freedom until he matures and becomes aware of the complexity and contradictory nature of male-female relationships in Moroccan society.

Jonathan Wright reviews

Al-Riwa'iyyun al-Iraqiyyun al-Yahud
(Iraqi Jewish Novelists)
by Khalida Hatim Alwan

Published by Mesopotamia Press,
Baghdad, 2015

The Arab Jews of Iraq

The past is a foreign country, they say, with good reason. Without constant reminders of how life was at a certain time in a certain place, it's easy to assume that it was just an earlier version of the present – without the trappings of modernity such as mobile phones, the Internet, cheap air travel and ready-made meals you can pick up from the supermarket and heat up in the microwave.

In the case of Baghdad and other Iraqi cities, the past even in the lifetimes of people alive today was a completely different place. On the eve of the Second World War, Baghdad alone had about 90,000 Jews, part of an Iraqi Jewish community that numbered more than 120,000 people. A third of the city's population was Jewish and many of them were prominent in public life – as politicians, lawyers, businessmen, educators and craftsmen in many trades. This was the largest and most influential concentration of Arab Jews in the world. I use the term "Arab Jews" deliberately, as some of them still do, because that was how most of them saw themselves. They were Jews by religion but Arabic was their mother tongue and often their only language, and they were fully integrated into the culture and civilisation that Marshall Hodgson called Islamicate – centred around Islam and Muslims but embracing a diverse range of subcultures.

Their world was turned upset and largely destroyed in the ten years between 1941 and 1951, and Baghdad was much diminished by the loss of them. By the mid-1950s only a few thousand Jews re-

د. خالدة حاتم علون

الروائيون
العراقيون اليهود

دراسة في الثقافة
والمنخيل والتجرب الروائي

mained and even that community continued to decline, until by the 21st century they were only a handful. Since large numbers of Jews had been living in Iraq for at least two thousand and several hundred years, the link between the disaster that befell them and the rise of Zionism in the first half of the 20th century, culminating in the creation of the state of Israel in 1948, is impossible to avoid. Local Iraqi politicians contributed to the disaster out of prejudice, greed and ignorance, mostly for short-term populist advantage.

Israel declared itself a state in May of that year and the Iraqi authorities responded within months with a succession of measures that made it increasingly difficult for Jews to live in the country. In March 1950 a new law gave Iraqi Jews a one-year opportunity to emigrate on condition that they relinquish their Iraqi citizenship and abandon most of the property. In its manifest injustice, the Iraqi government's treatment of the Jewish population almost equalled Israel's treatment of the Palestinians who stood in the way of a large Jewish state in Palestine, and the injustices that accompanied the massive displacements on the partition of India. Iraqi Jews dispersed widely but many of them joined an organised air lift that at one stage was taking 500 Iraqi Jews a day from Baghdad to Cyprus and then on to Israel.

Such a large group of people, many of them well educated through the French-financed schools of the Alliance Israelite Universelle, naturally included a number of writers, as well as younger people who would later feel driven to record their experiences in writing, often in fictional form. These writers are the subject of a thorough, 520-page overview of their literary production – *Iraqi Jewish Novelists* by

Khalida Hatim Alwan, published in Arabic by Mesopotamia Press in Baghdad.

They range from Samir Naqqash, a tragic genius who clung to his Iraqiness and to the Arabic language throughout his troubled and peripatetic life, to Sami Michael, who switched to Hebrew in the 1970s and found a place for himself in Israeli society, albeit as a leftist, a defender of civil rights and a critic of discrimination against Sephardic and Mizrahi Jews inside Israel. One of the writers,

Khalida Hatim Alwan

Naim Kattan, has spent very little time in Israel, moving in Montreal in 1954 and flourishing as a prolific writer in French on a variety of themes, not exclusively on his Iraqi heritage or memories. Yet another, Anwar Shaul, who was well established by the 1940s as a writer of short stories and of poetry in traditional styles, stayed on in Iraq despite the harassments and ran a printing business there until he finally gave up and moved to Israel in 1971 at the age of 67.

Alwan concentrates on the elements of commonality between them, such as the many references to Iraqi Jewish traditions and rituals in their works and their ideas about religious and national identity and "otherness". She also explores aspects of their literary technique, such as the way they incorporate poetry and references to music and other arts into their works.

She says this group of writers shared a certain set of beliefs about the status and role of the Jewish community in Iraq – that they had a right to live in Iraq, that they had made an important contribution to Iraqi national life, that Judaism was a religion that could and should be dissociated from the political ideology of Zionism and that the persecution of Jews in Iraq in the period shortly before and after the creation of Israel was a gross injustice that they needed to expose.

Communism was also a common theme because it transcended religion and offered Iraqi Jews equal status with members of all the country's other religions and sects. Several of the writers, especially

Samir Naqqash

Shimon Ballas

Sami Michael and Shimon Ballas, retained their communism as they tried to find a place in Israeli society.

But unfortunately Alwan's book tells us tantalisingly little about the men themselves (they are all men, as far as I can determine) or about the psychological effects of being uprooted at short notice from the society into which they were born and then being transported at short notice to an unfamiliar country where they did not know the language and where they were dominated by European Jews who often treated them as inferior relatives. Nor does she examine the thinking that determined why some writers continued to write in Arabic while others adopted Hebrew.

But the fact is that many of the writers showed an extraordinary and puzzling attachment to the language in which they were educated – standard literary Arabic, which was different from the colloquial Iraqi and the colloquial Judeo-Arabic that they would have spoken in the street and at home.

"I tried to write in Hebrew but my way of thinking is restricted to Arabic, which I have clung on to," said Isaac Bar Moshe, who served as an Israeli diplomat in Cairo in the 1980s after the Egyptian-Israeli peace treaty and wrote a lengthy memoir in Arabic of his childhood in Iraq. "It was my mother tongue. I was twenty-three when I left Iraq and I never found an alternative as a means of expression."

"Arabic is my language and I know no other language," said Samir

Naqqash, who did in fact speak Hebrew competently. "From the first moment I have lived within this shell. I have not been influenced by the Western culture that prevails in Israel and I have still not found its language. I arrived in Israel at the age of thirteen as an Iraqi Arab, and after fifty years I left it like my father, as a pure Arab."

Shimon Ballas, who adopted Hebrew as his medium of expression more readily than many of his fellow Iraqi Jewish writers, said that he did so mainly for practical reasons, rather than as part of adopting a new identity, as one might expect from someone who was in effect expelled from his native land by hostile forces. "I haven't forgotten Arabic. It's still a part of my cultural and spiritual identity although I've switched to writing in Hebrew for reasons that you well know, including the fact that I have to write for readers that understand the language I write in," he said.

In *Outcast**, his best-known work, published in English translation in 2007, Ballas hints at his ambivalent relationship with the country of his birth by fictionalising the life of Ahmed Soussa, an Iraqi Jew who converted to Islam and stayed on in Iraq after the massive exodus of the 1950s. The convert hero recalls how he wrote a letter to the London Times in 1930, arguing against denial of Islam and imitation of the West, and in favour of "Eastern peoples" maintaining their authentic identity as members of a different civilization, an essentially Muslim civilization which may, in time, take on some traits of Western civilization.

"I articulated an honest call to all Jews in the Arab East to emerge from their separatism and join shoulders with their Muslim and Christian brethren against Zionism. Jihad against the Jews? Only a mean, disfigured spirit could interpret my book that way. Not against them, but for their own good as human beings, I believed, and still do, that it was their duty to break free of the tribal concept, to shake off the ethnocentric and xenophobic mentality that characterizes Judaism, the same mentality that finds its vulgar and brutal expression in Zionism," the protagonist says.

Bar Moshe explained the ambivalence and even outright hostility of many leftist Iraqi Jews towards Judaism and Zionism thus: "They would say, 'I was brought up on Judaism, but I'm someone who has renounced his religion. I'm against religions. I'm disgusted by Judaism, but communism asserts, and I believe, that the communist system respects freedom of religion . . . That's why I tell you that

Sami Michael   Shmuel Moreh

Zionism is a fascist and iniquitous political movement that is hostile to religions and hostile to Judaism itself. I am an Iraqi before being a Jew.'"

Shalom Darwish, one of the older Iraqi Jewish writers, fled to Iran during the period of turmoil because he refused to go through the process organised by the Iraqi government, which required a renunciation of Iraqi nationality. "I saw renouncing my nationality as insulting. I had inherited it from my parents and my forefathers just as I had inherited the traits what ran in my blood . . . It wasn't a garment that I could put on and take off however or whenever I wanted or when it was asked of me by people whose forefathers had come to Iraq hundreds of years after mine."

Samir Naqqash was probably the most extreme case of antipathy towards Zionism, an attitude that was personal as well as ideological. "We came here (to Israel), and it was a very great disappointment," his sister, Samira Yosef, told Haaretz newspaper in remarks published in Naqqash's obituary in 2004. "We were very humiliated, and as a result, my father died very young, two years after our arrival. He died, like my brother, of cardiac arrest. We were in tents for the first two months, in the Sha'ar Ha'aliyah camp, and then spent a year and a half in tents in the Amishav camp, and then we were there for eight years in shacks, until they built apartment houses."

Naqqash never settled down. Aside from Israel, he lived at various times in Turkey, Iran, Lebanon, Egypt, India and England, but his only real home was an Iraq that no longer existed. Some of his work is extraordinary. He went to Egypt several times and met the great Egyptian writer Naguib Mahfouz. He then tried to settle down there, on the mistaken assumption he would be welcome, but it was not a happy experience.

"I warned him," said Professor Shmuel Moreh, the Iraqi-Israeli academic and writer who is in many ways the dean of the writer community. "I told him, it's a known fact that the Egyptians regard every foreigner as an enemy and a spy. But he told me, they appreciate me there very much. There I can live from my books like a king. What happened was that after three months he and the whole family returned here, because the Egyptians almost lynched him," said Moreh, quoted in Naqqash's obituary in *Haaretz*.

Moreh has been a driving force behind the Jerusalem-based Association for Jewish Academics from Iraq, which must count as one of the most unusual institutions in the Middle East, publishing thirty-four mainly literary works in Arabic between 1980 and 2007, apart from other works in Hebrew.

Inevitably those books were almost impossible to market in Arab countries and at home the audience for such works is shrinking year by year as Israelis of Iraqi origin lose touch with their parents' or grandparents' language and points of reference.

"It is very unlikely that in the foreseeable future new Jewish writers in Arabic, or dynamic (Jewish) communities using Arabic as their first language, are going to emerge. Fifteen hundred years of Judeo-Arabic speech, and nearly as many years of writing, in Hebrew or Arabic characters, are now nothing but past history," says Sassoon Somekh, writing on the website Sephardic Horizons.

* Extracts from Outcast *were published in* Banipal 21, Autumn 2004, *translated from the Hebrew by Amiel Alcalay, who wrote a commentary on the book and Ballas's works.* Outcast *was finally published in full in 2007 by City Lights Books, and was reviewed by Judith Kazantsis in* Banipal 31, Spring 2008. *The review is available to read online at http://www.banipal.co.uk/book_reviews/43/outcast-by-shimon-ballas/. A French edition entitled* Signes d'Automne, *translated from the Hebrew by Sylvie Cohen, was published by Samuel Shimon's Editions Gilgamesh in Paris in 1996*

Clare Roberts reviews

The Ninety-Ninth Floor
by Jana Fawaz El Hassan

Translated by Michelle Hartman

Published by Interlink Publishing, USA.
November 2016

ISBN: 9781566560542, pbk, 264pp,
$15.00 / £12.00

Running away
to New York

Lebanese journalist and novelist Jana Fawaz El Hassan's third novel, the first to be translated into English, is *The Ninety-Ninth Floor*. The novel is a frank look at love between two conflicting characters: their deep and divisive family roots, irreconcilable backgrounds, and the underlying forces that hold them together. Set in both New York and Lebanon, two worlds collide in the most painful, frustrating and fitful of ways.

Majd, the Palestinian protagonist, is a successful employee at a video game development company, working in a prestigious 99th floor office in Manhattan. Severely maimed in the Sabra and Shatila massacre of 1982, he moves to New York with his father for a new life, which, somewhat guiltily, he finds. Sporadic correspondence with his cousin Muhammad back "over there" in Shatila, in addition to his disability, keeps him acutely reminded of all he has left behind, and of the horrors his family faced in the massacre, an incident he will never – can never – forget.

It is perhaps this memory that renders remarkable his relationship with Lebanese dancer Hilda. As the relationship unfolds, the present intersperses with the past, with its memories of growing up in Lebanon re-emerging. Never far from the surface is the 1982 mas-

THE NINETY-NINTH FLOOR

Jana Fawaz El Hassan

translated by Michelle Hartman

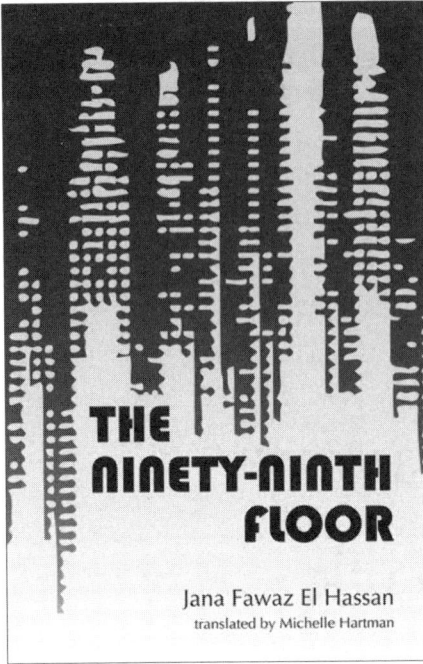

sacre: both Majd and Hilda have grown up in the fallout from this tragedy. Hilda, from a well-off, respected Christian Lebanese family, has had entirely different experiences of growing up in Lebanon, but she too has left for New York in search of a new beginning and new opportunities. Their love is unexpected and inexplicable, but binding. The relationship revealingly holds up a mirror – a theme running throughout the novel – to their individual selves and their pasts, prompting new questions and shining light on old truths. Pivotal to the novel is the effect of Hilda's decision to return to Mount Lebanon on her relationship with Majd. It is a decision fuelled by her desire to find answers to the most burning but buried questions of her past, even if the truth to be uncovered is far from being what she wants to hear. Back home, she is reminded that division and disunity pervade even the closest of family units. She learns that memories, however painful, cannot be bottled up and forgotten indefinitely. Waiting for her in New York, Majd is tormented by his love for her, suffocated, and can only think to punish her for her absence by rejecting her calls, only deepening the hole bored into his chest by her absence. Imagining Hilda with her family in Mount Lebanon, he is reminded of the atrocities he has left behind, his identity and life of exile questioned further.

An array of other characters also find in the city of New York a refuge from their painful pasts. Majd's friend, Mohsen, from the war generation, leaves his family behind in Lebanon, changing his name to Mike and revelling in his successful new life, "absorbed in promiscuity and drunkenness but at other times [drowning] in bouts of nostalgia". Eva, a beautiful Mexican woman, is also in New York to

Jana Fawaz El Hassan

escape her past. For Majd, New York, and his high-rise office block, represents the top – "every other place would be lower – Beirut and the Palestine [he'd] never known". High up in his tower block, he feels that he is "eternally running away towards greatness". Linking all the characters, in essence, is the sentiment that New York symbolises this running away.

In 2015 Jana Fawaz El Hassan received the accolade of being listed among the BBC's 100 Women for her taboo-breaking first novel *Forbidden Desires*, alongside such influential figures as Egyptian feminist writer and activist Nawal el-Sadaawi. Less ground-breaking, but nevertheless shortlisted for the 2015 IPAF Prize, is *The Ninety-Ninth Floor,* for its perceptive insight into growing up in post-civil war Lebanon, life in pre-2001 New York, and the feasibility of a relationship between two very different characters.

Susannah Tarbush reviews
**Trials of Arab Modernity:
Literary Affects and the
New Political
by Tarek El-Ariss**
Fordham University Press, New
York, 2013
ISBN: 978-0-8232-5171-1 (hbk);
978-0-8232-5172-8 (pbk); 248pp, hbk
$78.00, pbk $25.00 / £20.99, kindle
£20.99.

Arab literary modernity in performance

In this invigorating study Tarek El-Ariss challenges prevalent con-
ceptualisations of Arab modernity, both those that treat it as a
Western ideological project imposed by colonialism, and others
that understand it as a universal narrative of progress and innovation. He writes: "In dialogue with affect theory, deconstruction,
psychoanalysis, Michel Foucault, and Walter Benjamin, this book
interrogates the reading of modern Arabic literature through tele-
ological narrative of progress or anticolonial struggle."

He disputes the reading of Arab modernity (*hadatha*) as innovation
in relation to tradition (*ihdath*). He reframes it as a somatic condition, which takes shape through accidents and events (*ahdath*) emerg-
ing in and between Europe and the Arab world, the literary text and
political discourse.

El-Ariss is Associate Professor of Arabic and Comparative Literature at the University of Texas, Austin, and has a doctorate from Cor-
nell University. *Trials of Modernity* was named an Outstanding
Academic Title by Choices, the journal of the Association of College
and Research Libraries (ACRL), a division of the American Library
Association.

The book includes a wealth of references and sources from classical
and modern Arabic literature and thought, and contemporary theory

Tarek el-Ariss

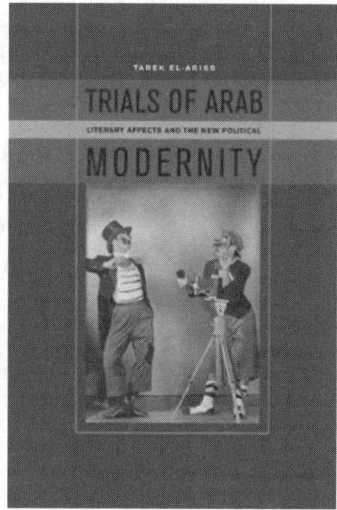

and philosophy. El-Ariss makes frequent reference to the work of other scholars in Arabic literature including Roger Allen, Muhsin al-Musawi, Sabry Hafez, Marilyn Booth, Samah Selim, Marie-Thérèse Abdel-Messih, and the late Radwa Ashour.

Rather than presenting an exhaustive account of Arab literary modernity, El-Ariss "offers close readings of specific encounters and texts" in which modernity is performed. And he bridges the gap between the Nahda – the "so-called Arab project of Enlightenment or Renaissance" and postcolonial and postmodern fiction.

El-Ariss is a persuasive and engaging writer. "Focusing on travellers and literary characters as they wander, run, take shelter, crouch, faint, panic, and go mad, I identify the simultaneous performances and contestations – or trials – of modernity in experiences and encounters in Cairo and London, in the interstices of the novel and the travelogue, writing and blogging," he writes.

Regarding the body as a site of rupture and signification his study "shifts the paradigm for the study of modernity in the Arab context from questions of representation and cultural exchange to an engagement with a genealogy of symptoms and effects. It traces a series of experiences and encounters arising from leaving home, aversion to food, disorientation, anxiety attacks, and physical collapse embodied in travelogues, novels, poetic fragments, and anecdotes from the nineteenth century to the present." His comparative approach allowed him "to identify a series of practices, rhythms, techniques, and encounters through which modernity becomes problematized, interrogated, tried out, and imagined."

El-Ariss has criticisms of the way in which Arab literature has sometimes been approached in US universities. For example, the teaching and translation of modern Arabic literature traditionally ignores current literary production and bypasses texts from the Nahda. "This perspective has reduced texts to sociological accounts and elided their literary complexity." Postcolonial studies often reduce Arabic texts to the practical politics of colonialism.

From the Nahda period, El-Ariss analyses in detail the travel narratives of the Egyptian Azharite imam and educational reformer Rifa'a Rafi' al-Tahtawi and the exiled Mount Lebanon intellectual Ahmad Faris al-Shidyaq. The works of both have become more available in English translation in recent years. Saqi in 2004 published *An Imam in Paris: Al-Tahtawi's Visit to France* (1826-1831), Daniel Newman's translation of the 1834 work *Takhlis al-Ibriz fi Talkhis Bariz aw l-Diwan al-Nafis bi-Iwan Baris*. Humphrey Davies's acclaimed translation of al-Shidyaq's *Al-Saq 'ala al-Saq* was published as *Leg Over Leg* by the Library of Arabic Literature in 2013.

Al Tahtawi wrote *Takhlis* after serving as spiritual guide for the first Egyptian student mission to Paris. El-Ariss reads his physical collapse, disorientation and hallucinations as "an embodiment of the encounter with modernity in nineteenth century Paris".

In his chapter on al-Shidyaq, entitled "Aversion to Civilisation", El-Ariss delves into *Kashf al-Mukhabba' 'an Funun Urubba* (Revealing the hidden in European arts). This was published in 1863 after al-Shidyaq had spent nine years in England and France.

Through its systematic interrogation of orientalism and colonialism, "Kashf dismantles, once and for all, the perceived passivity of the Nahda text, alleged receptacle of European ideas and cultural models". Al-Shidyaq exposes "civilization's inconsistencies and inherent contradictions" and deconstructs it through his abhorrence of English food. "In narrativizing the trials that constrain and poison him – food tastings, accidents and anxiety attacks – al-Shidyaq diagnoses civilization's violence to the body."

El-Ariss deals with the literary staging of colonialism in modern Arabic literature in his chapter on Sudanese writer Tayeb Salih's seminal 1963 novel *Season of Migration to the North*. He is unhappy with some of the ways in which the novel has customarily been treated in academia.

In the chapter entitled "Majnun Strikes Back" El-Ariss examines queer Arab sexuality in contemporary literature and "reads modernity's trials in fits of madness, disguise and collapse". He investigates the association of homosexuality with madness through two characters: the flamboyant Lebanese homosexual Samir in Lebanese author Hanan al-Shaykh's 2001 novel *Innaha London ya 'Azizi* (Pantheon published Catherine Cobham's translation *Only in London* in 2001) and rebellious 18-year-old gay Sayf in Egyptian writer Hamdi Abu Golayyel's 2002 novel *Lusus Mutaqa'idun* (Marilyn Booth's translation, *Thieves in Retirement*, was published by Syracuse University Press in 2006).

El-Ariss gives a compelling account of the new Arab literary scene in the chapter "Hacking the Modern". The advent of techno-writing in forms including blogging, chatting, e-mailing, texting and social media, has brought structural and linguistic transformation to Arabic literature. "Specifically, the encounter with the virtual and the effects of globalization are ushering in a new set of intertextual references that cut across languages, media and genres."

He describes Ahmed Alaidy's 2003 novel *An Takun 'Abbas al-'Abd* as an "iconoclastic manifesto of new writing" (the translation by Humphrey Davies was published by AUC Press as *Being Abbas el Abd* in 2006). El-Ariss notes that Alaidy's main target is authoritarian Arab regimes: "Examining acts of desecrating books and state institutions, I argue that Alaidy's new-generation antihero supplants the disoriented Arab traveller one finds in al-Shidyaq, al-Tahtawi, and al-Shaykh."

El-Ariss makes a link between the new Arabic literature and the Arab uprisings. He writes: "The affects in new texts, expressing anger and frustration, cannot be separated from the bodily affects generated by revolts from Tunisia to Syria from 2010 onward." And he argues that "a comparative analysis of contemporary fiction, Nahda, and diasporic and postcolonial texts serves to frame the social and political transformations associated with the Arab Spring".

Emma Branagan reviews

The Jasmine Sneeze

Authored and illustrated by Nadine Kaadan

Lantana Publishing, April 2016.
For ages 4-8 years, ISBN: 978-0-9932253-8-3,
pbk, size: 24cm2, 32pp, £6.99
Eformat: ISBN 978-0-9932253-9-0, £4.99.

A crafty cat is outwitted

Enter the colourful and sweet-smelling world of Haroun, the happiest cat in the world! He likes nothing better than snoozing next to fountains on the warm marble court-yards of the beautiful ancient city of Damascus. He listens to music by the moonlight and of course enjoys receiving treats from everyone! A life of company, abundant treats and freedom – what more could a cat want?

Of course, Haroun is not happy with what he has. There is something that he would like to get rid of. Something that seems to make everyone else happy but himself. Why do they love this thing so? Why do the people of Damascus treat it as a member of their family?

Watch Haroun in this superbly illustrated, clever and humorous book as he devises a crafty plan to eliminate the other long-standing resident of Damascus, the delightful and sweet smelling Jasmine. Is he prepared for the cheeky tricks that the Jasmine Spirit has in store for him? Is he prepared for the realisation that his life is intricately intertwined with hers and that of the people of Damascus?

I read *The Jasmine Sneeze* to my class of five and six-year-olds, and they were very interested to know where Damascus was. By chance we had also been on a class outing to the Royal Horticultural Society's Wisley Gardens earlier in the year and so everyone knew what jasmine smelt like, which made it a very animated reading.

The book's award-winning children's author and illustrator Nadine Kaadan is from Damascus herself and has published over 15 illustrated books for children in Arabic and English since starting to write at the age of eight.

CONTRIBUTORS

Monir Almajid was born in 1951 in Qamishli, Syria. He graduated from Damascus University in the Faculty of Fine Arts, and since 1969 has been a film critic, writing for Syrian and Arab media. After settling in Dennark in 1983, in 2008, he became editor of the Danish newspaper *Al Khabar*. *Qamishlo*, excerpted above, is his first novel.

Adil Babikir is a Sudanese translator into and out of English and Arabic, living in Abu Dhabi. He has translated two novels by Abdelaziz Baraka Sakin. and two anthologies – of poetry and short stories.

Liana Badr is a well-known Palestinian novelist, and short story writer, also a journalist, poet and cinema director. Born in 1950 in Jerusalem, she was raised in Jericho, studied at the University of Jordan, and graduated from the Beirut Arab University with a BA in philosophy and psychology. In 1979 she published her first novel *A compass for the sunflower* (English translation Women's Press, 1989). Since then she has published five novels, including *A Balcony over the Fakihani*, trans. Peter Clark and *The Eye of the Mirror*, trans. Samira Kawar, 4 collections of short stories, two poetry collections and four books of essays.

Paul Blezard is a broadcaster, writer, and presenter. He presented "Between the Lines", the author interview programme that helped Oneword Radio win two Sony Gold Awards. He is a Banipal trustee.

Emma Branagan is a junior school teacher interested in cross-cultural matters, who lived and worked in Italy for a number of years.

Peter Clark is a writer and cultural consultant on Middle East affairs. He has translated eight novels from Arabic and written several books, including *Damascus Diaries: Life under the Assads* (2015). He is a contributing editor of *Banipal* and a trustee.

Raphael Cohen is a translator based in Cairo and a contributing editor of *Banipal*. His translations of recent Arab fiction include Mona Prince's novel *So You May See* (2011), *Status: Emo* by Eslam Mosbah.

Laura Ferreri has a BA in interpreting and translation (Trieste University, Italy) and an MA in Arabic Translation (Edinburgh University, CASAW).

Jona Fras is a PhD candidate and teacher of Arabic in the Dept of Islamic and ME Studies at the University of Edinburgh.

Camilo Gomez-Rivas is a historian of the medieval Mediterranean. His PhD (Yale) was on Islamic law and society in the Maghreb. He translates poetry and is a contributing editor of *Banipal*.

Maha Hassan is a Syrian-Kurdish journalist and novelist. She was born in Aleppo, Syria, and has lived in France since 2004. Since 1995 she has published eight novels in Syria and Lebanon. In 2005, she was awarded a Hellman/Hammett grant for persecuted writers by Human Rights Watch. Her novel *Umbilical Cord* was longlisted for the 2011 IPAF and excerpted in *Banipal 44 – 12 women writers*.

Rosa Yassin Hassan is a Syrian novelist and writer. She was born in Damascus in 1974 and studied architecture at university. After graduating in 1998, she became a journalist for various Syrian and Arab periodicals. Her first published book was a short story collection *A Sky Tainted with Light* (2000). Her first novel was *Ebony* (2004), which won the Hanna Mina Prize. Her third, *Hurras al-Hawa* (Guardians of the Air, 2009), was longlisted for the 2010 IPAF. In 2009, Hassan was chosen as one of the Hay Festival's Beirut39, the 39 best Arab writers below the age of 40. Since 2012 she has lived in Germany.

Haitham Hussein is a Syrian Kurdish novelist, born in 1978 in Amuda in the province of Hasaka, Syria. He has published three novels, and works as a freelance journalist and literary critic for major Arab newspapers including *Al-Arab, Al-Hayat, Assafir*, and *Al Bayan*. In 2015, he founded a website about the Arabic novel, Alriwaya.net.

William Maynard Hutchins has translated many contemporary Arab authors including Naguib Mahfouz. He is a contributing editor of *Banipal*.

Julia Ihnatowicz is a freelance translator of Arabic. She lived and worked in the Middle East over several years and has an MA in translation (SOAS).

Nouri al-Jarrah is a Syrian poet, born in Damascus in 1956. He lived in Beirut since 1981, then Cyprus and, since 1986, in London as a journalist and editor. He has published over 14 collections of poetry, after his first (The Boy) in 1982 in Beirut.

Fawaz Kaderi was born in Deir Zour, Syria in 1956. He has been living in Munich, Germany, since fleeing Syria in 1999. In Syria he published six collections of poetry, and in Germany five more, the first, *Nelken in der Nacht* (2014), a bilingual edition.

Samira Kawar is a literary translator and an experienced energy journalist, and a TV and radio journalist. Her translations include *The Eye of the Mirror* by Liana Badr and Abdul Rahman Munif's *Story of a City: A Childhood in Amman*. She is a trustee of the Banipal Trust for Arab Literature.

Khaled Khalifa was born in Aleppo, Syria, in 1964 and holds a BA in Law from Aleppo University. He has written many successful screenplays for TV series and for the cinema and has written regularly for Arab newspapers. His third novel *In Praise of Hatred* (2006), was short-listed for the 2008 IPAF. His next, *No Knives in the Kitchens of this City* (English edition 2016), won the 2013 Naguib Mahfouz Medal and was shortlisted for the 2014 IPAF.

Abderrahim Elkhassar is a poet, born in Asfi, Morocco, in 1975. In 2009 he was selected as one of the Hay Festival's Beirut39 authors, the 39 best Arab writers below the age of 40.

Luke Leafgren is an Assistant Dean and Arabic instructor at Harvard University, where he received his PhD in Comparative Literature in 2012. He has translated two of Mushin al-Ramli's novels, *Dates on my Fingers* and *The President's Gardens* (excerpted above) and *Oh Salam!* by Najwa Barakat.

Becki Maddock has a 1st class BA in Arabic and Spanish (Exeter University), and working knowledge of other languages including Persian and Dari. She is presently pursuing an MA at SOAS, London.

Nada Menzalji is a poet from Lattakia, Syria. She studied at Tishreen University there. She works for *Jazeera* magazine as an editor, and lives in London.

Hala Mohammad is a Syrian poet and filmmaker, born in Lattakia. She studied film-making in Paris and worked as a costume designer for two well-known Syrian films, al-Lail and Sandouq al-Dunya. Since 1994 she has published nine collections of poetry. She has lived in Paris since 2011.

Rasha Omran was born in Tartus, Syria, in 1964. She has a degree in Arabic literature from Damascus University. She was the director of Al-Sindiyan festival of culture until civil war closed it down. She has published several collections of poetry and lives now in Cairo, Egypt, working as a journalist.

John Peate is a translator, teacher, researcher and language consultant based in the UK. He has BAs in English and in Arabic from Leeds University, an MA in Translation from SOAS, London and a PhD in Arabic Linguistics from the University of Salford.

Leri Price is an Arabic-English translator based in the UK. Her translation of *In Praise of Hatred* by Khaled Khalifa was long-listed for the Independent Foreign Fiction Prize.

Muhsin Al-Ramli was born in the village of Sudara in northern Iraq in 1967. He is a writer, poet, academic and translator and has lived in Madrid, Spain, since 1995, where he has published 11 works – collections of short stories, novels, a play, essays and poetry). He has a PhD in Philosophy and Spanish Literature from the Autonomous University of Madrid (2003), and teaches at the Saint Louis University, Madrid.

Clare Roberts has a BA in Arabic and Islamic Studies (Oxford University) and an MA in Arabic Poetry and Turkish Politics (SOAS, London). She works at a charity, and reviews for *Banipal*.

Olivia Snaije is a journalist and has covered the Middle East for the past twenty years. She writes for *Publishing Perspectives* and reviews for *Banipal*.

Paul Starkey is Emeritus Professor of Arabic at Durham University and Vice-President of BRISMES. He has translated many works by contemporary Arab authors, and won the 2015 Saif Ghobash Banipal Prize for Youssef Rakha's *The Book of the Sultan's Seal* (Interlink, 2014). He is a contributing editor of *Banipal* and chair of the Banipal Trust.

Susannah Tarbush is a freelance journalist specialising in cultural affairs in the Middle East. She writes the Tanjara blog, and is a consulting editor of *Banipal* and regular reviewer.

Valentina Viene is Italian by birth, now settled in the UK. She has a BA in Arabic and English from the University of Naples L'Orientale, and an MA in the Theory and Practice of Arabic Translation.

Dima Wannous was born in 1982 in Damascus. She is a writer and translator and studied French literature at Damascus University and the Sorbonne. She caught the eye of literary critics with *Tafasil* (Details, 2007), her first short story collection, published in Damascus. Her debut novel (The Chair) came out in 2008. In 2009, she was selected as one of the Hay Festival's Beirut39, the 39 best Arab writers below the age of 40.

Jonathan Wright is a translator who worked for many years as a journalist in countries across the Arab world. His translations include three IPAF winners, Raja Alem's *The Dove's Necklace* (2011), Saud Alsanousi's *The Bamboo Stalk* (2013), and Youssef Ziedan's *Azazeel* (2012) which was joint winner of the 2013 Saif Ghobash Banipal Prize.

FLEMISH AUTHORS

Fikry El Azzouzi (b. 1978) is a Flemish-Moroccan author who debuted in 2010 with the novel *Het Schapenfeest* (The Feast of the Sheep), the story of eleven-year-old Ayoub, who has to go with his father to help slaughter a sheep for the Feast of the Sacrifice, but devises the most inventive strategies to avoid doing so. He is also a columnist and writes for theatre. For *Drarrie in the Night* and for his play *Reizen Jihad* (Jihad Travels), El Azzouzi was awarded the 65th Ark Prize of the Free Word, an award presented to an author notable for his or her individuality and boldness.

Roderik Six (b. 1979) is a literary journalist and columnist for the weekly magazine *Knack*. His debut novel *Vloed* (Flood) struck like lightning and was awarded, among others, the Bronze Owl for the best Dutch language debut. In 2014 he published *De boekendokter* (The Book Doctor), an acclaimed collaboration with his now sadly deceased colleague and friend, Thomas Blondeau. He has also published numerous short stories in literary magazines at home and abroad. *Val* (Fall, 2015) is his second novel.

Bart Van der Straeten (b. 1979) studied Dutch Language and Literature at the University of Ghent and is still connected to his alma mater as a lecturer. In 2014 he made his poetry debut with the publication of *Onbalans* (Imbalance) at publishing house Vrijdag. The collection, which was highly praised upon publication, contains poems that try to avert an existential crisis by a very well-built structure. In *Onbalans* uncertainty is taken for granted. In pure, naked and deep verses, the poet tries to assess the probability of the truth.

Tom Van de Voorde was born in Ghent, Belgium in 1974. He is a writer, curator of interdisciplinary projects and translator of American poetry into Dutch. In 2008, he published his first book of poetry, a collection of "contemporary landscape" pieces, entitled *Vliesgevels filter* (Curtain walls filter). In 2013 his second collection *Liefde en aarde* (Love and earth) was awarded the tri-annual poetry prize of East Flanders, with selected poems translated into ten languages and in 2016, the full collection published in Swedish translation by Ramus Forlag. A collection in Arabic translation is forthcoming from Almutawassit Press. In 2010, Tom was appointed curator for literature programmess at the Centre of Fine Arts, BOZAR, in Brussels.

Charlotte Van den Broeck (b. 1991) holds an MA in English-German language and literature and is now studying Verbal Arts at the Antwerp conservatory. She twice reached the top 100 of the Turing National Poetry Prize and published in *Het Liegend Konijn, de Revisor, das Magazin* and *DWB*. She is already a household name as a performance poet. In 2015, with her debut volume *Kameleon* (Chameleon), she was added to the line-up of the Saint Amour tour through Belgium and the Netherlands. She performed her works at the official opening of the Flanders-Netherlands as Guest of Honour at the 2016 Frankfurt Book Fair.

Kathleen Vereecken (b. 1962) is a freelance journalist known for her fiction and nonfiction writing for children and young adults. She made her debut in 1993. Since her fourth book she has written mostly historical youth novels. Vereecken paints a convincing and almost sensorial portrait of the age, embedded in a meticulous structure that keeps the reader engaged. Her work has been translated into French, German, Italian, Korean and other languages. *Hair* is her first novel for adults.

GUEST LITERATURE TRANSLATORS

Astrid Alben is a poet, editor and translator. Her debut collection *Ai! Ai! Pianissimo* was published by Arc Publications (2011). Her poems, essays, translations and reviews are widely published including in the *TLS, Granta* and the *Best of British Poetry Anthology 2015* (Salt). Alben is the editor of three art/science anthologies, all published by Lars Müller Publications. Alben is a FRSA and a Rijksakademie and Wellcome Trust Fellow and artistic director of PARS, www.parsfoundation.com. To hear her poems visit www.astridalben.com.

Michele Hutchison was born in the UK in 1972 and has lived in Amsterdam since 2004 with her Dutch husband and two children. She was educated at UEA, Cambridge, and Lyon universities. She translates literary fiction and nonfiction, poetry, graphic novels, and children's books, most recently *La Superba* by Ilja Leonard Pfeijffer, *Roxy* by Esther Gerritsen, and *Fortunate Slaves* by Tom Lanoye.

Brian Doyle (Scotland, 1956) has translated several books from Dutch into English in addition to teaching at the University of Leuven in Belgium. Recent projects include Jef Geeraerts' *The Public Prosecutor* (2009), Jacqueline van Maarsen's *Inheriting Anne Frank* (2010), Christiaan Weijts' *The Window Dresser* (2010), Tessa de Loo's *The Book of Doubt* (2011), Paul Glaser's *Dancing with the Enemy* (2012), and Bob Van Laerhoven's *Baudelaire's Revenge* (2014). He is also responsible for *The Square of Revenge* (2012), *The Midas Murders* (2013), and *From Bruges with Love* (2015), the first three novels in Pieter Aspe's "Detective Van In" series.

Anna Asbury studied Classics and Linguistics at Cambridge University, then found her way into literary translation through a summer course with the Dutch Foundation for Literature, which she stumbled across during her PhD studies in linguistics in Utrecht. On her return to the UK she set herself up as a freelance translator. Recent work includes several books on politics and economics, the graphic novel Rembrandt, about the life of the artist Rembrandt, blogs and articles about Flemish and Dutch culture for *The Low Countries Yearbook* published by Ons Erfdeel, and a handful of books on business ethics and popular psychology for self-publishing authors.